Praise for *Can I say that?*

'*Can I Say That?* is a bold, provocative, responsible, and deeply wise guide to understanding – and navigating – DEI in today's world in flux. Poornima's hard-earned insights and perspective are gifts for humanity – and a brighter future for all!'

April Rinne, Futurist, advisor and author of *Flux: 8 Superpowers for Thriving in Constant Change*

'One of the few books I've read on diversity, equity and inclusion that has made me stop and think about what it takes to be a truly inclusive leader. Poornima's approach to the subject is incredibly thought provoking and has challenged me to look at my learned values and belief systems and the way I have led. I would recommend this book to any leader who is serious about DEI and initiating real change in both their own mindset and, more importantly, the culture of their organisation.'

Abu Bundu-Kamara, Senior Director, Global Inclusion and Diversity, Expedia Group

'Poornima is a world class thought leader on the topic of DEI. Her approach invites and inspires everyone to play a role in creating inclusive spaces for all.'

Alero Akuya, Vice President, Global Brand, the LEGO Group

'Once again, Dr Luthra delivers an invaluable take on the topic of DEI with great provocations and insights to help drive progress and meaningful impact.'

Angela Taha Naef, PhD, Chief Research and Development Officer, Reckitt

'A groundbreaking guide that cuts through the noise and illuminates the path to inclusivity. Essential reading for anyone committed to meaningful change with inspiring and deeply practical advice.'

Astrid Warmington Sundberg, Executive Director, Operation Smile, Norway

'*Can I Say That?* brilliantly unpacks the universal challenge of fear and offers invaluable insights on overcoming it to communicate, engage and lead with true inclusivity. This is a must-read for anyone—and especially for leaders—who want to cultivate a more courageous and connected workplace in today's diverse, dynamic world.'

Chisom Udeze, Executive Director, Diversify

'In this candid and insightful book, Poornima Luthra masterfully uncovers how fear drives resistance to DEI initiatives and provides a practical roadmap for overcoming it. Drawing from extensive interviews and real-world experience, she addresses the uncomfortable truths about workplace inclusion with empathy and wisdom, creating an essential guide for anyone seeking to make meaningful change in their organisation.'

Des Dearlove and Stuart Crainer, Co-founders, Thinkers50

'True understanding can only be achieved through curious and courageous communication. This book shows us how to build bridges in a divided world.'

Heather Hansen, author of *Unmuted*

'*Can I say that?* encourages us all to confront our fears and embrace DEI as an opportunity. It's a particularly important guide for those in STEM fields that lack adequate representation. I can say that it is very timely given the need for diverse thinking to drive inclusive innovation that our world needs!'

Jayshree Seth, Chief Science Advocate and Corporate Scientist, 3M

'A must-read and a powerful call to face and transcend fear, filled with profound insights and practical guidance to elevate your DEI agenda.'

Kogulan Kugathasan, DEI lead, Simcorp

'If you've ever faced or found resistance to DEI, this is the book for you! Dr Poornima Luthra expertly and emphatically guides us through common concerns and questions on this important subject. *Can I Say That?* presents data-backed, actionable solutions such as harnessing the power of curiosity and navigating discomfort. A must-read for all!'

Ruchika T. Malhotra, author of *Inclusion on Purpose* and *Uncompete*

'The first step towards DEI is embracing the fear that DEI invokes. *Can I Say That?* is a research-based and empathetic guide to help you take the first step – and the many that follow.'

Sara Louise Muhr, PhD (she/her), professor of Diversity and Leadership, Copenhagen Business School

'A bold, essential guide that cuts through the fear surrounding DEI and offers actionable steps for true inclusion. Luthra converts skeptics and emboldens champions of change.'

Selena Rezvani, Wall Street Journal bestselling author of *Quick Confidence: Be Authentic, Boost Connections, and Make Bold Bets on Yourself*

'An outstanding book with self-reflective tools and approaches to overcome the fear of change, empowering us to break free from constraints caused by fear and enabling us to avoid repeating the past.'

Sumit Sudan, Managing Partner, Deloitte, Denmark; audit, L&C

'Yet another thought provoking book from Dr Poornima! This book provides highly relevant data and research, whilst also taking you on a personal journey to reflect on human reactions that may hinder your organisations from really being able to move the DEI needle. This is certainly a book every leader, DEI practitioner and employee should read.'

Winta Negassi, Head of HR, LCS, Google, Northern Europe

Can I Say That?

Pearson

At Pearson, we have a simple mission: to help people make more of their lives through learning.

We combine innovative learning technology with trusted content and educational expertise to provide engaging and effective learning experiences that serve people wherever and whenever they are learning.

From classroom to boardroom, our curriculum materials, digital learning tools and testing programmes help to educate millions of people worldwide – more than any other private enterprise.

Every day our work helps learning flourish, and wherever learning flourishes, so do people.

To learn more, please visit us at **www.pearson.com**

Can I Say That?

Your go-to guide for Diversity, Equity and Inclusion

Poornima Luthra

Pearson

Harlow, England • London • New York • Boston • San Francisco • Toronto • Sydney
Dubai • Singapore • Hong Kong • Tokyo • Seoul • Taipei • New Delhi
Cape Town • São Paulo • Mexico City • Madrid • Amsterdam • Munich • Paris • Milan

PEARSON EDUCATION LIMITED
KAO Two
KAO Park
Harlow CM17 9NA
United Kingdom
Tel: +44 (0)1279 623623
Web: www.pearson.com

First edition published 2025 (print and electronic)

© Pearson Education Limited 2025 (print and electronic)

ISBN: 978-1-292-73713-3 (print)
        978-1-292-46908-9 (ePub)

British Library Cataloguing-in-Publication Data
A catalogue record for the print edition is available from the British Library

Library of Congress Cataloging-in-Publication Data
Names: Luthra, Poornima, author.
Title: Can I say that? : your go-to guide for diversity, equity and inclusion / Poornima Luthra.
Description: First edition. | Harlow, England ; New York : Pearson, 2025. | Includes bibliographical
references and index. | Summary: "In an era marked by rapid social and organisational change, the
imperative for diversity, equity and inclusion (DEI) stands as a beacon for forward-thinking leaders. We
live in a world increasingly characterised as BANI - brittle, anxious, nonlinear and incomprehensible.
This descriptor aptly captures the volatile and unpredictable nature of our global environment, where
traditional approaches often fail, and resilience is continually tested. The skills and behaviours of
inclusive leadership are crucial in navigating this BANI world, enabling organisations to be more
adaptable, empathetic and coherent - even midst chaos. While deeply unsettling, this environment
is inviting each of us to grow, evolve and transform into leaders for a new age. But what holds us back
from seizing this opportunity? When I first had the pleasure of meeting Poornima, we connected
immediately around a passion to understand the concept of fear - a powerful driver, and derailer, of
change and progress. And I am so grateful that she decided to create in this book a space for deep
exploration of why we seem stymied because of it, and how to get unstuck. Poornima's writing shines a
light on the discomfort we have both felt personally, as early voices for change and often the only voices
for it, and as professionals who now coach leaders and organisations on its impact. We both share the
belief that, if we don't solve for fear, so universal and yet so individually experienced, it will diminish
and destroy the fabric not only of workplaces, but society. This book is one of the first that's put this
necessary discussion front and centre"-- Provided by publisher.
Identifiers: LCCN 2024061401 (print) | LCCN 2024061402 (ebook) | ISBN 9781292737133 (paperback) |
ISBN 9781292469089 (epub)
Subjects: LCSH: Leadership. | Social change. | Equality.
Classification: LCC HM1261 .L87 2025 (print) | LCC HM1261 (ebook) | DDC 303.3/4--dc23/eng/20250214
LC record available at https://lccn.loc.gov/2024061401
LC ebook record available at https://lccn.loc.gov/2024061402

10 9 8 7 6 5 4 3 2 1
29 28 27 26 25

Cover designer Two Associates
All the illustrations in the book are by Poornima Luthra

Print edition typeset in 10/14 Charter ITC Pro by Straive
Print edition printed and bound by Bell & Bain Ltd, Glasgow

NOTE THAT ANY PAGE CROSS REFERENCES REFER TO THE PRINT EDITION

For

All of us who experience fear

For

My children, their generation and the generations to come

For

My DEI community who inspire me every day with their commitment, resilience and perseverance

While we work hard to present unbiased, fully accessible content, we want to hear from you about any concerns or needs with this Pearson product so that we can investigate and address them:

- Please contact us with concerns about any potential bias at https://www.pearson.com/report-bias.html.

- For accessibility-related issues, such as using assistive technology with Pearson products, alternative text requests, or accessibility documentation, email the Pearson Disability Support team at **disability.support@pearson.com**.

Contents

—

Contents

About the author

Dr Poornima Luthra (she/her) is a recognised author, keynote speaker, business consultant and leading practitioner-academic in the field of talent management and Diversity, Equity and Inclusion (DEI). She is the author of *Leading Through Bias* (December 2023), *The Art of Active Allyship* (November 2022) and *Diversifying Diversity* (May 2021).

Photo by Liv Latricia Habel

As associate professor at the Copenhagen Business School, she provides effective DEI thought-leadership from a global perspective, workshops and consultancy services for organisations who are determined to nurture inclusive workplaces for their diverse talent. She was ranked as one of the world's 30 up-and-coming management thinkers by the prestigious Thinkers50 in 2023.

Learn more at https://poornimaluthra.com/.

Acknowledgements

I am so grateful for the immense support I have received from many people in my life. This work is challenging and, without this support, it would be very difficult to continue on this pathway of wanting to make organisations more diverse, equitable and inclusive.

Our childhood experiences shape us. As a child, I grew up hearing my father saying 'expand, expand, expand [your circles of influence]'. My father and my mother continue to live these words in their very actions, positively influencing a continuously growing number of people in their lives. Mom and Dad, I am truly grateful to you both for planting this seed of wanting to positively influence others and being such amazing role models.

Writing a book is a very immerse journey and the people closest to us are often deeply affected by it. Tanuj, my darling partner in life, you have been my rock all these years – thank you for so enthusiastically supporting me even when I become 'Authorzilla' and disappear into the cave to write. To my loves, Rohan and Tejas, thank you for choosing me to be your Mama, and for challenging me to be the best version of myself for you.

To all my fellow DEI practitioners, you inspire me. We all know how tough this work is and how emotionally draining it can be. On those tough days when I experience fear, you are the ones who give me the strength to continue. To all whom I have had the pleasure of engaging with on this topic, thank you for the deep and powerful conversations. To all the leaders, workshop participants, keynote attendees and students, thank you for engaging honestly and openly with me; for asking the tough questions that challenge me to do better.

Most importantly, a heartfelt thank you to each of you who so courageously shared your fears with me that form the foundation of this book, to those who took the time to offer feedback on the draft manuscript, and to Jennifer for writing the foreword. This book would not have been possible without all of you.

I feel so grateful to have found my ikigai to do the work that I love, that the world needs, that I am good at and that I can be paid for.

Foreword

By Jennifer Brown

In an era marked by rapid social and organisational change, the imperative for diversity, equity and inclusion (DEI) stands as a beacon for forward-thinking leaders. We live in a world increasingly characterised as BANI – brittle, anxious, nonlinear and incomprehensible. This descriptor aptly captures the volatile and unpredictable nature of our global environment, where traditional approaches often fail, and resilience is continually tested.

The skills and behaviours of inclusive leadership are crucial in navigating this BANI world, enabling organisations to be more adaptable, empathetic and coherent – even amidst chaos.

While deeply unsettling, this environment is inviting each of us to grow, evolve and transform into leaders for a new age. But what holds us back from seizing this opportunity?

When I first had the pleasure of meeting Poornima, we connected immediately around a passion to understand the concept of fear – a powerful driver, and derailer, of change and progress. And I am so grateful that she decided to create in this book a space for deep exploration of why we seem stymied because of it, and how to get unstuck. Poornima's writing shines a light on the discomfort we have both felt personally, as early voices for change and often the only voices for it, and as professionals who now coach leaders and organisations on its impact. We both share the belief that, if we don't solve for fear, so universal and yet so individually experienced, it will diminish and destroy the fabric not only of workplaces, but society. This book is one of the first that's put this necessary discussion front and centre.

With nearly 25 years in the DEI space, I know that as much as I teach behaviours and strategies, they will never truly stick or be absorbed if we're spending our energy protecting ourselves from each other, mistrusting motives and sidelining empathy and compassion as 'nice to haves' or 'business-irrelevant' – or worse, wanting to return to 'the way it was'. I think of Peter Drucker's famous quote that reminds us: 'Culture eats strategy for breakfast' – which asks us then to consider, are we building cultures of high trust or cultures of fear around us? What do we want our legacy to be? I remember this each time I take a leap of faith with an audience, when I come out on stages globally as a member of the LGBTQ+ community. I lead with my story of stepping into the light and, yes, trusting others with my truth. I decided this was more important than fear.

Our macro-environment today is unfortunately heightening a culture of fear; we're living through an unprecedented backlash to organisations that have remained dedicated to the concepts of empathy and equity for all. This is of course not new – but fear of change, fear of the unknown and fear of lost privileges are powerful fuel when wielded by the powerful. The backlash happening now several years after the start of the pandemic and the murder of George Floyd is an attempt to force a cancellation – which I predict will not be lasting – of organisations' efforts to update their cultures for an emerging future. Anyone in business, with customers and employees, knows that demographics are destiny – and outdated ways of working and relating to one another simply won't work anymore. Embracing DEI is an existential necessity rather than a mere ethical choice.

Poornima has made this wonderful point to me in our conversations that backlash is a powerful signal that the status quo is being disrupted – which also signals that there is a powerful disturbance being created. For every action, there is a reaction. In a BANI environment, opportunities for change are all around us. If you've picked up this book, you're likely unsettled enough to be asking big questions, about your role, how to use your voice, access and other forms of capital and how to shift the systems around you. Whether you experience fear when speaking up, worry about backlash or the discomfort of sharing truths that might be hard for others to hear, or fear about 'getting it wrong' or inadvertently causing offense, recognising and remembering it as a universal driver that we all share offers a profound basis for empathy and connection.

The antidote to fear is a learning culture. One that gives space and grace to each other, that invites humble reflection, experimentation, and can tolerate imperfection, knowing it's an important ingredient of growth. I think we can all relate to the deep desire to be seen and supported as we learn, as we tell the truth, as we puzzle through the shifting landscape around us and as we develop new language and skills.

I love this book for the way it skilfully outlines methods to confront and convert this resistance into constructive dialogue and, ultimately, acceptance. And I find it deeply comforting how Poornima emphasises that the pushback we witness today is not just a momentary challenge but a part of a larger evolutionary process within organisations.

Let this book inspire you, challenge you, and guide you as you play your part in shaping a more inclusive world.

Jennifer Brown

Inclusive leadership expert and best-selling author, *How to be an Inclusive Leader: Your Role in Creating Cultures of Belonging Where Everyone Can Thrive* and podcast host, *The Will to Change*.

Author's note

It had been weeks of interruptions, tone policing, aggressive language and plain rudeness that had been directed at me as chair of a board.

In the beginning, I dismissed it. I even gaslit myself, thinking that 'it must be me'. 'Try a different style of communicating,' I said to myself.

I questioned my leadership capabilities and accessed resources to help me deal with 'difficult colleagues'. I sought out ways to fix myself and make myself more 'likeable'.

I began to walk a tightrope, watching what I said or did so as not to come across as aggressive or bossy when, in fact, I was just being assertive, a quality required of someone in a leadership role.

No matter what I did, the behaviour persisted, and it was targeted – at me – the only non-white person on the board.

In one message, I was referred to only as 'P', followed by a list of tasks that were divided up across a few board members. That might not sound out of the ordinary, except for the fact that everyone else was referred to by their full name, all Anglo-Saxon, many with the same number of letters as my own. When I addressed it, I was told I was making too big a deal out of it. The person in question insisted they simply didn't have the time to spell out my name. Yet, apparently, they had the time to spell out the names of everyone else.

The one time that I addressed the problematic behaviour of certain board members, I was met with vocal opposition. I was told that I had no right to speak to them that way. Thankfully, other board members – allies – stepped in to support what I was saying.

This behaviour went on for months.

I knew what I was experiencing was wrong. I knew how it made me feel. I wanted to address it more concretely. I wanted to call it out.

But I couldn't and I didn't. I felt helpless and anxious.

I kept asking myself – *Can I say that?* – and I kept second-guessing what would happen if I did. Could I tell this person that what they said was discriminatory or tell them how their actions made me feel? 'Can I say that?' is a question I hear time and time again, usually from people who wanted to know if they were being biased or offensive. Here I was asking the question in a different – but related – context.

When I finally decided that I needed to get some support, my leadership coach asked me – 'What is holding you back? What are you fearful of?'

There it was. The word I was dreading – *fear*.

It made me pause and reflect. Could it be that my hesitancy and resistance to address what was happening was because of fear? I work in the diversity, equity and inclusion (DEI) space and frequently advise others on how to navigate the exact situation I was facing myself and yet I was fearful of addressing the toxic non-inclusive behaviours around me. I was fearful of being seen as the 'over-sensitive brown woman' who can't handle push-back; the woman who isn't 'strong' enough . . . who lacks real leadership skills . . . you get the picture. I was worried about how I would be perceived if I addressed the discrimination at play in how I was being spoken to and being treated. The more I thought about it, the more convinced I was that it was fear that was holding me back.

A few weeks after my conversation with my leadership coach, I was at one of my favourite art museums, the Louisiana Museum of Modern

Art in Denmark for the Icelandic artist Ragnar Kjartansson's exhibition, entitled 'Epic Waste of Love and Understanding'. As I walked into the exhibit, I was met with a row of pepper shakers labelled 'Fear'. Surely, this was a sign that the idea of fear was something I needed to dig deeper into.

And so, I did.

When I started to look around, it was clear that I wasn't the only one who was hesitant to address bias and nurture inclusion. There was plenty of evidence in the form of news headlines and social media posts of resistance and backlash, from all sides – those outside of the DEI field, and those – like me – who were in it; those who were being discriminated against and those who were being discriminatory. There was definitely a change in the tide from the summer of 2020 when, globally, organisations spurred by the Black Lives Matter movement began their most committed efforts towards DEI, to the vocal political and business backlash and resistance to DEI that we have seen in the past two years. It seemed like DEI was facing an existential crisis.

I was keen to understand why – why were so many exhibiting signs of resistance and backlash, and why were they so anti-DEI? After my own experience, I could not help but wonder if fear had anything to do with it. Despite the question my leadership coach had asked me, I was hesitant to assume that fear was at the core of the growing backlash to DEI efforts. I needed proof. And so, my research began. Through it, it became clear that the root cause of the resistance and backlash that we are experiencing and witnessing towards DEI is fear. But here is the thing – fear is a strong emotion, and we are often fearful of fear itself. At the same time, it is the elephant in the room. Our fear of fear is holding us back from making progress towards inclusive, fair and representative workplaces.

If we draw on the immense body of knowledge on psychology and neuroscience, we know that fear occurs in response to a threat. The threat here is DEI initiatives. But what aspects of DEI initiatives do we see as a threat? What are people fearful of when it comes to DEI initiatives? These questions were exactly what my research sought to unpack and understand, to go deeper into understanding this fear so that we can let go of it. The outcome of my research is this book, *Can I Say That?*

'Can I say that?' is a phrase that I have heard countless times before; and thought of myself. Perhaps you have too. It reflects the emotions of worry, anxiety and nervousness that so many of us experience when engaging with the topic of DEI. Too many of us are scared and hesitant to engage in DEI topics – worried about being cancelled, anxious when attending DEI events, and nervous about making cultural and systemic change happen.

Can I Say That? is not a prescriptive book that will tell you what you can or cannot say. It goes much deeper than that to address the root cause of why we are even asking ourselves that question – fear. So, if you are looking for a book that will be give you the 'easy fixes', then this is not that book. This book will need you to go deeper, to confront and let go of your own fears and to transform the way you look at DEI – from seeing it as a threat to seeing it as a wonder opportunity for your workplace and society. This book is your go-to guide to making this transformation in you happen.

Who is this book for?

I am a believer in the positive intent of people. I believe that the vast majority of people want to do better. We want to be a part of creating organisations that are diverse, equitable and inclusive, but so many of us are fearful of engaging.

Making our workplaces more representative, fair and inclusive requires everyone to play their role in making it happen. To enable a cultural transformation, we need to let go of our fear. In the words of Nigerian author Chimamanda Ngozi Adichie: 'Culture does not make people. People make culture.'[1] Cultural transformation cannot happen without everyone being on board – leaders and employees. It needs us all to step up. So, you don't have to work in HR. You don't have to have a formal title or be a business leader. You don't have to be a chief diversity officer. Regardless of formal title, we all have a sphere of influence in our organisations – we can influence upwards, downwards, sideways with peers and external stakeholders and, importantly, we can influence ourselves. Each one of us needs to let go of our fear to nurture inclusive spaces within our own spheres of influence.

So, if you are:

- the sceptic who doesn't believe in DEI and thinks, 'Why should I care if it doesn't directly affect me?'
- the HR/DEI practitioner who is fearful of the backlash and of not being able to make enough of a positive impact
- the business leader who wants to do good but doesn't want to get it wrong, or
- the individual employee who finds DEI topics and initiatives uncomfortable and threatening, but realises they have no choice and wants to know what to do,

then this book is for you.

How to use this book

This book aims to be your go-to guide for Diversity, Equity and Inclusion by focusing on understanding and providing a guide to let go of your fear of DEI. This book aims to cut through the noise to provide a rich understanding of what DEI actually means, and how each one of us can make our workplaces more inclusive, fair and diverse. In doing so, we will develop our emotional intelligence which, in turn, will enable the cultural transformation required to build inclusive workplace cultures.

While I firmly believe that systemic change is needed in conjunction with cultural transformation, I feel that a lot has been written about systemic change including in my own prior books, and so, here, I chose to focus on what is needed to enable the cultural transformation necessary to create organisations that are more representative, fair and inclusive. Our organisational systems, structures, policies and practices are built, upheld and modified by us – people. To move us from where we are today, we need to focus on cultural transformation to drive systemic change through a mindset shift. While the focus of this book is on organisational contexts, much of the content can be applied to contexts outside the workplace as well.

The first two chapters of this book set the stage for what is to come, taking stock of DEI and the backlash and resistance towards DEI. While much of the headlines that make it to the news come from a US/UK context, I try and provide a picture that this backlash and resistance is experienced in many parts of the world. In Chapter 3, I share with you my research into understanding the emotions that cause this backlash and resistance, focusing on the core emotion of fear. This research is the foundation of this book. If you enjoy knowing the research that led to this book, then this is the chapter for you. If not, a quick skim of the chapter may suffice. You can always come back to this chapter later on. Chapters 4 to 7 provide a guide for what we can do to help us let go of our fears to stop seeing DEI as a threat. Each of these chapters provides practical nudges and tools to help us embrace DEI and make the cultural transformation happen. These chapters build on each other and contain self-reflection exercises as well as examples to guide your journey. It would be helpful to have a notebook for these exercises to make note of your responses and to come back to them as needed. You may also do this on your phone or laptop, if preferred. If there is a chapter that resonates more with your current needs, you could start there and then continue with the others. If not, my recommendation would be to follow the order in which the chapters are laid out. I end this book with sharing a personal experience and my own journey to convey that this is a journey of continuous progress.

This book is about enabling a mindset shift in you – to let go of your fears and inhibitions to embrace diversity, drive equity and nurture inclusion. This mindset, a fearlessly inclusive mindset, is what I believe is needed to move the needle. The nudges presented here are grounded in the Knowledge-Attitude-Behaviour (KAB)[2] approach that guides much of my work in this space. In order for us to embrace

DEI, we need to develop our understanding of the issues at hand (Knowledge), reflect on our biases and the ways in which we engage with others (Attitude) and act in ways that level the playing field and nurture inclusion (Behaviour).

This book is based on my research exploring the resistance and backlash to DEI. At the start of each nudge, you will find a quote from an interviewee who shared their view on the resistance and backlash to DEI. Their identities have been anonymised and their quotes edited only for readability. The nudges presented provide a guide for us all. They are based on the data collected and years of working with individuals, teams and leaders of global organisations to nurture inclusion, diversity and equity in their workplaces. I share with you what I believe works. Of course, context matters. Not all of the nudges work as effectively in your context, so focus on those that *do* while modifying others to suit your contextual needs. Think of these nudges as suggestions for what actions you may wish to take. Reading this book is the first step, but the real work of putting these nudges into practice is what really matters. The good news is that it is entirely in your control.

Be open-minded and reflective to explore your own fears. There will be moments of discomfort and I ask you to sit with the discomfort. Resist the temptation to brush it off or suppress it. Discomfort drives change. I ask you to be brutally honest with yourself. You don't need to share your reflections with others but please be honest with yourself. As you begin to learn about the forms that fear takes, you may begin to recognise these fears in others. Approach them with empathy. Focus on creating spaces for honest and open conversations. As you read, I invite you to approach these pages from a place of curiosity. An increased awareness of fear of DEI is not meant to point fingers or shame those who experience fear. Let's be honest, we all experience fear of DEI. Even those of us who tirelessly work in this space.

By the time you reach the end of this book, my hope is that you will be able to recognise the fears of DEI in yourself and others. My hope is that you see this as a positive experience; that once you know your fears, you can work towards letting them go. And my hope is that you make sincere efforts to let go of the fear of DEI. This journey to embrace DEI will take time and you may feel sometimes that you are taking one step forward and two steps back. This is a human journey of ups and downs. Think of DEI as a muscle that you are trying to strengthen – it requires consistent effort.

I am on this journey with you. I don't claim to have all the answers. I am sharing what I believe is a set of best practices that we can engage in to confront our resistance to DEI head on – to get to the core – and let go of the fear that holds us back. I invite you to join this journey with me.

Poornima

Chapter 1

——

Taking stock of DEI

What is equity? Isn't that a finance term? Shouldn't the 'E' refer to equality?

When we have people who are different, it feels like we end up with more miscommunication and conflict. How is that a good thing?

We are a group of very similar people, but we have very positive inclusion scores. Isn't that a good thing?

From boardrooms to newspaper headlines, Diversity, Equity and Inclusion (DEI) is everywhere you look. In many organisations, you are likely to find DEI topics being discussed and, in some organisations, you may come across bias awareness training being conducted.

Today, DEI is a key pillar of the people strategy of many organisations and institutions.

But what is DEI?

Broadly speaking, DEI refers to a strategy or approach, and associated activities and initiatives, taken to nurture inclusive and fair workplaces for the diversity of human beings.

The term itself can be traced back to the mid-1960s, a time when social movements and legal changes were reshaping the world. Like many words or terms that have been around for decades, semantic change can occur. Meanings or connotations are added, altered or removed, sometimes resulting in a modern meaning that is radically different from the original usage. There is also a risk, particularly with acronyms, of becoming a 'buzz word' or jargon, fashionable in a particular context or point in time and used without a true understanding of the actual or intended meaning of the individual words.

This is certainly true with DEI, a term that is widely used but not always in a way that reflects its original meaning and, increasingly, with negative connotations. DEI is assumed to be a political issue when, in fact, it has been politicised. Instead of letting an acronym become the villain, we need to recentre the conversation around the actual principles of diversity, equity and inclusion.

Understanding DEI

For as long as human beings have existed, there has been diversity. As humans, we have a deep desire to feel included and to be treated fairly. We want to show up as ourselves and feel that we belong.[3] With that in mind, we can – and should – consider Diversity, Equity and Inclusion (DEI) a fundamental and integral part of the human experience.

The acronym DEI takes many forms across different contexts and cultures, with the letters being combined in many ways. Some may know it as EDI or IDE. For others it may be I&D or D&I. And for yet others, there may be additional alphabets to form DEIB or DEIBJ. At the core of each are the main components of diversity (D), equity (E) and inclusion (I), with belonging (B) and justice (J) used more explicitly in certain contexts though implicitly understood in DEI. In this book, for simplicity, I shall refer to it as DEI as an encompassing term for all these various possible combinations of the letters.

While the acronym, in its various forms, may have gained widespread awareness, there is a desperate need to go back to the basics and move away from the complicated jargon, misunderstanding and misinterpretation that exists today. We need clarity as to what Diversity, Equity and Inclusion mean at their very core.

Diversity

> ## Diversity
>
> Diversity refers to the 'presence and participation of individuals with varying backgrounds and perspectives, including those who have been traditionally underrepresented'.[4]

When we refer to diversity, we refer to the myriad of human differences in perspectives, backgrounds and experience that should be represented in our workplaces. In my book, *Diversifying Diversity,* I introduce the idea of a diversity thumbprint that all of us have. This thumbprint is made up of multiple dimensions of diversity that include – among others – gender, sexual orientation, age, disabilities, educational background, neurodivergence, race, ethnicity, religion, marital and parenthood choices and socio-economic backgrounds. Some of these dimensions are visible while others are invisible; some can even be both. These dimensions intersect or weave together to form our own unique identity. It is important to emphasise that this intersectional view of diversity is fundamental to understanding diversity in its truest sense. Very often, the focus of diversity in our workplaces is on singular dimensions. For example, organisations focus on women or marginalised ethnic groups or the LGBTQ+ community. Women are not a monolith, and neither is any other group. In her pivotal work on intersectionality, Professor Kimberlé Crenshaw emphasised that we don't experience our world through one dimension at a time. We experience the world around us, including our workplaces, through our intersectional identity.[5]

Intersectionality

Intersectionality is 'an analytical framework for understanding how aspects of a person's social and political identities combine to create different modes of discrimination and privilege'.[6]

I often hear this: 'We may look homogenous in terms of the visible dimensions of diversity, but we actually have diversity of thought – we are from different universities and industries.' This line of reasoning is a sign of complacency and an excuse used to justify the lack of diverse representation across a range of intersectional visible and invisible dimensions in a homogenous group and should not be mistaken for diversity of thought. When we refer to diversity of thought, we are referring to the different viewpoints and perspectives that arise from not only the invisible dimensions of education or personality but also from the visible dimensions of people's identities, including their backgrounds and culture. Diversity of thought is far more likely when we have visible diversity. While diversity refers to this intersectional representation and ensuring that the diversity of human beings have a seat at the table, representation alone is not enough. We also need equity and inclusion. This means expanding the table to include more seats and even modifying or redesigning the table to make the table fairer and more inclusive.

Equity

Why equity and not equality, and what's the difference anyway? *Equality* assumes that everyone is the same and experiences the world in the same way. This includes their path through education, healthcare and societal systems, as well as the workplace. We know that this is not true. There is plenty of evidence (which we will explore later on in this chapter) that illustrates that marginalised identities continue to experience discrimination in and outside our workplaces. Given this, our focus needs to be on equity – on levelling the playing field so that, across intersectional identities, there is greater fairness and justice.

Equity

Equity refers to 'equal access to opportunities and fair, just, and impartial treatment'.[7]

From a workplace perspective, equity is the practice of giving all employees equal access to opportunities for employment, development and career advancement. A key aspect of equity is fairness – fairness not just for me and others 'like me' but fairness for all. Equity is about ensuring that there is fairness in (1) the processes and procedures through which a decision is made (procedural justice) and in (2) the interpersonal relationships between managers and employees, especially when exchanging information, conveying decisions, asking for input, delivering feedback or resolving conflicts (interactional justice).

Achieving equity does not happen automatically. It requires individuals and leaders in organisations to make concrete efforts to address the inequity and correct the bias in systems, structures, policies and practices. In an inequitable world, equity can be seen as a disruption, inconvenience and even oppression by those who have and continue to benefit from the inequity.

Are our workplaces fair?

To reflect on whether our workplaces are indeed fair or not, ask yourself the following questions and pen down your thoughts in your notebook:

- 'Is treating everyone the same actually fair?'
- 'In our workplace, are we applying an approach that works for one particular group assuming that it works for everyone else?'
- 'If our goal is to get the best out of each and every team member, will a one-size-fits-all approach actually work?'

Next, engage in conversations with your colleagues, team members and manager about these topics to hear other people's views. Try and reach out to colleagues who come from different backgrounds and life experiences compared to yourself. Resist the temptation to assert your views during those conversations. Instead, listen with the intention to understand how others view this topic, rather than to respond.

Finally, reflect on what you have heard. Have your views changed upon hearing other people's perspectives? Write down the top three things that you have learnt – or perhaps unlearnt – about fairness in the workplace in your notebook.

Inclusion

> **Inclusion**
>
> Inclusion is 'a sense of belonging in an environment where all feel welcomed, accepted, and respected'.[8]

According to Lynn M. Shore and her colleagues from San Diego State University, for inclusion to be felt, two key components need to be present – people need to be valued for their uniqueness and they need to feel that they belong.[9] Inclusion is the feeling you have when you are a part of the larger group with a shared sense of purpose – be that your team, function or organisation as a whole – that motivates you to participate, and that your unique talents and perspectives are sought, respected and valued. From an employee perspective, inclusion is (1) being accepted and treated equally regardless of their identities, (2) being integrated into decision making and (3) being able to express themselves authentically.[10] In a culture of inclusion, everyone can openly share the aspects of identity that they wish to share, while not feeling the need to cover up or hide parts of their identity. In such a culture, people feel safe and welcome to be who they are, while also feeling like they belong.

It is important to note that inclusion is not felt in a DEI strategy or roadmap; it is felt in our day-to-day interactions with each other – by the coffee machine, at lunch and during meetings. To nurture inclusion requires active allyship. In my book, *The Art of Active Allyship*, I define allyship as the 'lifelong process of building and nurturing supportive relationships with under-represented, marginalised or discriminated individuals or groups with the aim of advancing inclusion'. Most of us are passive allies. We may believe in DEI, but we don't engage actively in it. It is not sufficient to say that we don't condone racism and sexism, for example. We need to be actively anti-racist and anti-sexist: anti-discrimination. To be an active ally, we need to engage in frequent and consistent behaviours that advance inclusion.

It is easy to assume that we are inclusive, especially when there is homogeneity among team members or in a workplace. After all, it is easier for people to be themselves and feel a sense of belonging when everyone else is 'like them'. This is not the kind of inclusion we are referring to here. True inclusion happens when the organisation and team are representative of the diversity of societies and customers across an intersectional range of dimensions of diversity, and where each person can be themselves with a deep sense of belonging.

Why is inclusion important? A June 2024 report by BCG based on a survey of 11,000 desk-based and frontline workers in eight countries, found that 48% of the respondents were dealing with the symptoms of burnout which they define as 'a state of exhaustion characterized by disenchantment with one's job and a sense of inefficiency'.[11] In India, the number was higher at 58% while, in Germany and Japan, it was at 37%. Their research showed that, while burnout has historically been considered to be a consequence of long hours, a physically demanding job, or a high-stress environment, it is also highly correlated with low feelings of inclusion. The report also highlighted that the four factors that have the greatest impact on employees' overall sense of inclusion are: good access to resources, senior managerial support, psychological safety with direct manager and fair and equal opportunity for success.

What DEI is and is not

The fundamental purpose of DEI is to foster fairness and inclusion. DEI efforts should empower everyone with the opportunities to succeed. In a workplace context, this means that DEI efforts need to address historic systemic, and cultural bias, and discrimination so that employees from marginalised groups have the same access to opportunities as their peers. DEI is an approach to nurture fairer workplaces in which people of different backgrounds feel included by addressing the inequity in organisational systems and culture. In doing so, DEI efforts ensure that organisations are reflective and representative of the diversity of society.

DEI is often understood too narrowly and we need to adopt a more holistic approach to DEI. DEI should be embedded in all aspects (systems, structures, policies, practices and culture) of organisational life, and requires long-term commitment to make systemic and cultural change. We will not make the progress that is needed if DEI focuses on 'quick fixes'. It is not limited to improving representation of women and other marginalised groups. DEI work is about improving the culture and systems of the whole organisation – to make them fairer. When DEI is done right, everybody benefits.

DEI

DEI is:	DEI is not:
a fundamental aspect of the human need to feel welcomed, valued and supported	an ideology
the right thing to do	charity
about addressing systemic and cultural biases	about attacking or replacing privileged identities
about creating a level playing field	a zero-sum game where one group gains at the expense of others
about redefining our understanding of what 'qualified' means	about hiring 'less qualified' candidates
about empowering people to lift and create space for others	about making people feel shame and guilt
everybody's responsibility	just for leadership or HR (human resources) to 'solve'

Historic systemic, and cultural, bias has led to groups of people that have greater power and advantages or privilege compared to others. Through no direct actions of their own, certain groups of individuals have had a smoother path to success, perhaps without even realising it. Others face barriers even to get on the path and, once there, they face bumps and boulders, making it more difficult or slower to move ahead. DEI aims to correct this unfairness to make our workplaces fairer and to give everyone access to the same obstacle-free path.

Workplace DEI initiatives

DEI initiatives are the 'practices aimed at improving the workplace experiences and outcomes of groups that face disadvantages in society'.[12] The origins of today's global DEI initiatives in the workplace can be traced back to the mid-1960s in the USA. The civil rights movement and Stonewall uprising provided the catalyst for DEI efforts in society and workplaces. At the same time, the introduction of equal employment laws and affirmative action marked the beginning of workplace diversity training. In the1980s and 1990s, globalisation marked a significant shift in DEI programmes, moving beyond the initial focus on racial issues and gender equality to embrace a broader spectrum of diversity, emphasising the business case for DEI efforts. In the 2000s, in response to changing demographics of the workforce, DEI strategies began to significantly influence corporate culture; DEI was no longer simply 'nice-to-have', but a business imperative with organisations creating DEI roles and departments. The modern form of DEI has gained momentum since 2017 in response to both the #MeToo movement and the resurgence of the Black Lives Matter movement.

Since 2020, DEI efforts have evolved significantly. Organisations have made strides in embedding their DEI into their business. In many, there has been a shift from viewing DEI as a human resources activity to one that focuses on impact through environment, social and governance (ESG) priorities. As we have seen earlier, leaders have also begun to realise that inclusion is not felt in a DEI strategy or roadmap, but in our personal interactions with each other – and addressing and empowering personal action through allyship will be a key focus area moving forward. One of the most significant shifts is the move away from a very narrow view of diversity to a wider and more intersectional view. There is an increase in global conversations around non-binary and transgender identities, ethnicity and race, age and sexual orientation among others, and companies are using self-identification surveys to collect employee data to create DEI activities to address the intersectional needs in their organisations.

Some of the common activities that form workplace DEI efforts include the following: openly stating the organisation's commitment to DEI in its mission statement; DEI strategy development; target setting; action plans and roadmaps to implement the company's DEI strategy; inclusion policy development; DEI awareness building, unconscious bias and leadership training programmes; Employee Resource Groups (ERGs); implementation of inclusive talent management practices across the entire employee life cycle; inclusive employer rebranding and marketing campaigns; roll-out of engagement surveys with inclusion components; mentorship programmes; implementation of inclusive design processes; as well as organising, donating to or taking part in DEI-related events and causes like Pride Month or International Women's Day. Some of these activities address the need for systemic change while others focus on cultural transformation, and some do both. However, many others are more performative and in place to pacify employees or external stakeholders by making it look like the organisation supports DEI. These do nothing more than provide symptomatic solutions to what are cultural and systemic problems; much like putting a band aid on a wound without treating the wound itself. These are what Mita Mallick, author of the book, *Reimagine Inclusion: Debunking 13 Myths to Transform Your Workplace*, refers to as *diversity dressing* which is the 'showcasing, presenting and amplifying diversity of representation when your workforce, products, or services aren't actually inclusive and are lacking in diversity of representation'.[13] An example of this is including photos of employees from underrepresented groups in social media posts or on your careers website that give the illusion of more workforce diversity than you have.

So, have these DEI initiatives led to progress?

Has progress been made?

I am often asked to provide success stories of companies or asked to name companies that are doing well on the DEI front. I always hesitate. Becoming diverse, equitable and inclusive is a complex endeavour that requires significant systemic and cultural transformation. While there are many companies that are certainly doing well on this front, what works in their context may not work in others. Also, how does one define success in this field? Different organisations may have different focus areas as per their needs and hence different metrics that they use to measure success. Yes, we can look at representation of identity groups and inclusion scores on employee engagement surveys, but they are both very limited in providing a full picture. It is also important to note that companies' scores in these aspects change over time when people leave and new people are hired, or when priorities change with leadership changes and shifting business conditions. So, let us look at some broader measures of progress.

Globally, the metrics used to measure progress look promising. A 2023 Workday survey across 19 countries found that 97% of companies have at least one DEI initiative while 78% said that the importance of DEI has increased over the past year. The number of companies with a dedicated budget for DEI rose from 76% in 2022 to 85% in 2023 with 45% of those foreseeing an increase in budget.[14] The majority of respondents to the survey also believed that DEI is having a positive impact on business outcomes, having the biggest influence on engagement, with 74% of respondents saying they have seen an impact, followed by belonging and inclusion, health and well-being, performance and retention.

The same survey found that US organisations are motivated to continue their DEI efforts due to business success and results from attracting and recruiting a diverse workforce and promoting employees from underrepresented backgrounds. Executives are increasingly examining the impacts of DEI on their businesses. In 2022, just 23% of US organisations were measuring the business impacts of DEI. That number increased to 82% a year later. The survey results also showed a maturing of DEI efforts with a growing focus on integrating DEI across business functions. The survey also exposes the challenge of measuring DEI efforts. While almost half of organisations measure diversity (49%), only 39% are able to track progress on employee inclusion and belonging.

A survey report released in January 2024 based on 320 C-suite executives across the USA found that, despite an increasingly challenging environment for diversity-related initiatives, 57% say their organisations expanded their IE&D commitments and level of activity in 2023, even while nearly the same proportion (59%) believed that the backlash towards corporate diversity programmes had increased. More than a third of organisations surveyed (36%) had maintained their IE&D efforts, while just 1% reported a significant decrease.[15] Another survey on the current state of workplace DEI efforts by the Institute for Corporate Productivity (i4cp) showed that 75% of the professionals surveyed reported that their companies are making progress[16] and only 9% of respondents said their organisations have failed to make progress towards their DEI goals over the past 18 months. Seems good so far, doesn't it?

There is more evidence of progress. A survey of 325 business leaders of companies headquartered in the USA by Morning Consult in January 2024 showed that 82% of business executives think diversity initiatives are critical to their business strategies, and 67% said they expect these efforts to become more important in the coming years.[17] The survey also showed that nearly half of executives said their primary reason for implementing diversity initiatives was to improve business performance, acquire better talent (43%) and increase creativity (38%). Only 2% of business leaders surveyed said such initiatives were not important. A December 2023 survey by The Conference Board of nearly 200 US chief human resource officers (CHROs) showed that none of the respondents planned to reduce their DEI initiatives, policies or programming while 63% planned to focus their efforts on attracting diverse employees.[18]

This progress is not just in the USA. DEI programmes in organisations in Asia[19] and Europe are growing as well. BCG's 2023 survey asked more than 6,000 employees in six Southeast Asian countries about their company's DEI programmes and their overall experience.[20] In this heterogeneous region of 680 million people comprising more than 1,500 ethnic groups, 43% of respondents said that their companies had diversity programmes, up from 36% in 2020. In the European Union (EU), DEI is seen as a driving force for social transformation and economic opportunity with multiple legislative frameworks in place to address discrimination in workplaces. These include the EU

Directive on Work-Life Balance for Parents and Carers, The European Accessibility Act and the EU Directive on the Gender Balance on Corporate Boards. These have a profound influence on the increasing pace of DEI efforts in organisations in the EU.

You may be tempted to look at the data on the progress being made and say to yourself, 'It isn't that bad.' While the data we have looked at so far paints a rather optimistic picture, it is not complete. Yes, some progress most certainly has been made, but it has been limited. Despite continual efforts for greater representation and inclusion in the workplace, there remains a significant underrepresentation in leadership positions in certain industries with pervasive discrimination still at play and we see tokenism masquerading as progress without actual cultural and systemic transformation. There is plenty of data that shows that the DEI efforts so far have been limited in achieving representation, equity and inclusion.

Following is a brief overview to give you an idea of where progress has been limited in some of the more visible aspects of diversity. It is well documented[21] that the challenges across visible and invisible dimensions of diversity are pervasive, so the following section is by no means exhaustive but is intended to illustrate that, while some progress has been made, many significant challenges remain.

Gender identity and sexual orientation

Every year, the World Economic Report provides data on how long it will take to achieve gender parity. In 2024, it will take 131 years to achieve global gender parity, which means that it will take generations before we see that become a reality. A poll by King's College London's Global Institute for Women's Leadership[22] across 31 countries shows that over half of people (54%) believe that, when it comes to giving women equal rights, things have gone far enough in their country with men more likely than women to agree with this statement (60% vs 49%). Over half of men (53%) agreed that, in promoting women's equality, we are discriminating against men compared to two in five women (39%).

What about in our workplaces? Let's begin at the top. Globally, women are not adequately represented in leadership. In 2023, just 7% of CEOs leading the largest publicly listed companies were women. Out of companies on the Fortune 500 list, women made up just 10% of CEOs.[23] An analysis of 1,100 companies in 2023 by S&P Global Sustainable1[24] shows that women hold about one-quarter (25.1%) of senior management or leadership roles, only slightly up from previous years. This lack of gender parity in both senior and junior management roles is despite the fact that, in more than 100 countries, women outnumber men in advanced education, suggesting there is no shortage of women in the talent pipeline. The glass ceiling is real.

While we have seen some progress in the science, technology, engineering or mathematics (STEM) sector, especially in countries like India where women constitute 43% of enrolment in STEM courses in 2024,[25] the progress for women through the corporate hierarchy remains a challenge. Women in STEM currently account for 29.4% of entry-level workers but only for 12.4% of C-suite executives.[26] Progress is similarly slow in the boardroom. Women hold about one-quarter (24.9%) of board positions globally[27] despite shareholder pressure for more gender-diverse boards and both company-driven and legislative quotas mandating women on boards.

It isn't just the glass ceiling women have to contend with. There is also the glass cliff, a term coined by Michelle Ryan and Alex Haslam, of the University of Exeter. This term refers to the real-world phenomenon in which women are more likely to be appointed to precarious leadership positions in poorly performing organisations, while men are more likely to be appointed to stable leadership positions in successful organisations.[28] Without the support, power, respect, time and other resources necessary to succeed in the role, especially in a time of crisis, these women are set up to fail.[29] Almost a quarter of women CEOs lasted less than two years in the role, and were twice as likely as men to leave their role within the first two years and four times as likely as men to leave within 12 months.[30] This is amplified for women of colour who face a particularly high level of scrutiny, aggression and a lack of empathy, making it harder for them to perform at their full potential.[31] In an HBR

Ideacast podcast interview with Sophie Williams, the author of *The Glass Cliff: Why Women in Power Are Undermined – And How to Fight Back*, Sophie emphasises that, alongside women, the glass cliff is also experienced by other underrepresented groups, including men of colour.[32]

Even in female-dominated industries, men dominate senior leadership positions at a disproportionate level compared to the gender mix further down in the hierarchy. Men in these positions hold more power and resources, and even earn more money.[33] This is what sociologist, Christine Williams, refers to as the 'glass escalator'. Her research shows that men in female-dominated occupations often experience a faster and smoother rise to the upper levels of leadership than women.[34]

And then we have the 'broken rung'. In McKinsey & Co.'s 2023 'Women in the Workplace Report',[35] women, and especially women of colour, remain underrepresented across the corporate pipeline. The main challenge facing women is reaching their first step in management, as opposed to higher up the ladder. This 'broken rung' was identified as the biggest hurdle women face on the road to senior leadership. In 2023, for every 100 men promoted from entry level to manager, 87 women were promoted. For women of colour, the number was only 73, down from previous years.

Yet, even factoring in glass ceilings, cliffs and escalators, as well as broken rungs, the picture is not complete. The 2024 Deloitte's 'Women @ Work: A Global Outlook' report[36] highlights that women experience persistent non-inclusive behaviours, ranging from sexual harassment to microaggressions, which are biases that are subtle and indirect, often hidden in humour, casual comments and even compliments. This is especially true for underrepresented groups. 16% have been harassed or made to feel uncomfortable by customers or clients and nearly one in ten has been harassed by a colleague. 31% report experiencing microaggressions that include being interrupted, 4% sexual harassment and 8% other forms of harassment in the prior 12 months. Further, a quarter of women say that people in senior positions in their organisations have made inappropriate actions or comments towards them.

There is plenty of evidence that shows that, while women do face significantly greater biases and microaggressions in the workplace, men can experience them too. In certain fields like human resources (HR), early years teaching as well as in nursing, men face biases based on the perceived qualities needed for those roles. For example, in HR, being 'warm' and 'personable' with higher emotional intelligence are characteristics that are seen as being integral to success. Also, stay-at-home dads and men taking their share of parental leave are often met with confusion and disbelief that they would want to take care of the children. They face stigmas from colleagues and family members alike. Even dads who show an active interest in their family – who leave work to pick up their children from school, watch their child play basketball or are involved in household chores – are not spared the stigma. Some are seen by others as 'weak' or not having what it takes to be a leader in the organisation.

LGBTQ+

If we look at the enthusiastic participation and sponsorship of many large global companies each June, when annual Pride parades take place, we may be fooled as to the amount of progress that has been made in workplace inclusion for the LGBTQ+ community. The data shows otherwise. Globally, about 40% of LGBTQ+ employees are closeted at work and 75% have reported experiencing negative day-to-day workplace interactions related to their LGBTQ+ identity in the past year.[37] 36% of employees who have come out of the closet have lied or 'covered' parts of their identities at work in the past year, while 54% of employees who are out at work remain closeted to their clients and customers.[38] Even in a country like Denmark, where there is an assumption of greater inclusion for the LGBTQ+ community, 81% of LGBT+ respondents have been exposed to or witnessed discriminatory situations at work.[39]

The 2019 Glassdoor Diversity and Inclusion Study was conducted in the USA, UK, France and Germany.[40] When compared to the other countries in the study, the percentage of employees reporting having experienced or witnessed workplace discrimination related to LGBTQ+ identity was highest in the USA at 33% compared to the UK (25%), France (22%) and Germany (15%). Among US employees, one in three (33%) has experienced or witnessed LGBTQ+ discrimination at work. The study also showed that, in the USA, younger employees (43% of ages 18–34) are more likely than older employees (18% of ages 55+) to have experienced or witnessed LGBTQ+ discrimination. In addition, employed LGBTQ+ identified men (38%) are more likely than employed LGBTQ+ identified women (28%) to have experienced or witnessed discrimination at work. When it comes to LGBTQ+ discrimination among younger workers, specifically, younger employed LGBTQ+ identified men (51% of aged 18–34) are significantly more likely than younger employed LGBTQ+ identified women (34% of aged 18–34) to have experienced or witnessed it.

What about the impact on the LGBTQ+ community of companies rolling back on DEI efforts? A survey in 2024 from LGBTQ+ advocacy group Human Rights Campaign (HRC) found that these rollbacks could negatively impact how the companies are perceived by the LGBTQ+ community. 72% of respondents said their employer rolling back its DEI efforts would make them feel less included or accepted, and 19.6% said they would either quit or start looking for another job.[41]

Race, ethnicity, culture, nationality and religion

As of 2024, black CEO representation on the Fortune 500 is just 1.6%.[42] In the UK, 18% of the population is of an ethnic minority, yet only 11.34% of FTSE 100 CEOs are from an ethnic minority background.

The EU European Agency for Fundamental Rights released a report in 2023[43] that painted a bleak picture of what it is like to be black in the EU. 45% of respondents say they experienced racial discrimination in the five years before the survey, an increase compared to 2018. In Germany and Austria, the number is over 70%. 34% felt racially discriminated against when looking for a job and 31% at work, with many likely to be offered temporary contracts for which they are overqualified.

In Estonia, refugees from African countries who identified as Muslim have experienced direct racism and exploitation by their employers, colleagues and clients, more so than other groups. In Hungary, one in five Roma surveyed in 2015 said they had experienced discrimination in the workplace. In Ireland, a large proportion of racist incidents reported are in the workplace (31%). In 40% of the cases reported, the victim's ethnic background was Muslim, followed by African (33%).[44]

Race bias begins very early on in the talent acquisition process. In the USA, candidates with 'non-European' sounding names send approximately 50% more applications than those with 'European' sounding names to get to the interview stage, even with the same skills.[45] In a study researching job applications in the UK, researchers applied for over 3,000 jobs, using names from various ethnic backgrounds. Otherwise, CVS and cover letters were identical. The study showed that only 15% of CVS with 'ethnic sounding' names received a callback compared to 24% of those with 'white sounding' names. The study also showed that applicants from an ethnic background had to send 60% more applications to get as many callbacks as the white majority, and that British employers were the most discriminatory. In Belgium, job applicants with foreign sounding names have a 30% less chance of being invited to a job interview compared to applicants with a similar profile but Flemish sounding names.[46]

A 2016 study showed that minority job applicants who 'whiten' their resumés by altering any information that indicates their ethnicity are more than twice as likely to receive a callback than those who do not.[47] During the two-year study, 1,600 fictitious resumés were sent to 16 different metropolitan areas in the USA. Some resumés were left as is, whereas others were 'whitened'. When African American names and experiences were unaltered, 10% of them received a callback. However, when African American candidates' resumés were 'whitened', that number jumped to 25.5%. For Asian applicants, 21% heard back if they changed their resumé, and only 11.5% of candidates did if their resumés were not 'whitened'.

It isn't just names, but also the 'ethnic accent' in which a language is spoken. In a survey in 2022, almost half of UK workers have had their accents mocked, criticised or singled out in a social setting. 31% of university students indicated that they were worried that their accents could have a negative impact on their future careers while 46% of workers have faced insults about their accents, with 25% reporting jokes at work.[48]

Age

Of biases witnessed or experienced by respondents, age topped the list.[49] According to a WHO analysis, about 50% of people in the world are assumed to hold age bias against older people. Several research studies have demonstrated age discrimination against older people, where age has been associated with lack of energy, competence and willingness to 'put in the work'.[50] Older workers with the same qualifications as younger peers often receive lower subjective evaluations on performance in job interviews or in job performance reviews.[51]

At the same time, a 2019 Diversity and Inclusion Study by Glassdoor in the USA, UK, France and Germany showed that younger employees (52% of ages 18–34) are more likely than older employees (39% of ages 55+) to have witnessed or experienced ageism.[52]

Disabilities

Despite legal protections for those who are physically disabled, as a group they remain underrepresented in our workplaces. In 2018, only 29% of working-age Americans with disabilities (between ages 16 and 64) participated in the workforce, compared with 75% of Americans without a disability. In 2018, there were 15.1 million people of working age living with disabilities in the USA and a report by Accenture suggested that, if companies embrace disability inclusion, they would have access to a new talent pool of more than 10.7 million people.[53]

A 2023 report by Nifty of 50 constituent companies in India shows that just 5 out of the 50 companies have more than 1% of Persons with Disabilities (PwDs) on their rolls, with four of them being public sector companies.[54] This is despite the 2016 Rights of Persons with Disabilities Act that requires 4% of all jobs in the public sector being earmarked for disabled people. It is estimated that there are between 40 and 90 million disabled people in India which makes up about 4%–8% of the population.[55] Data from the National Centre for Promotion of Employment for Disabled People reveals that less than 1% of India's educational institutions are disabled-friendly, less than 40% of school buildings have ramps and just 17% have accessible restrooms, making it challenging for disabled people to access education in order to enter the workforce.[56]

In the UK, the progress is notable. In 2019, over 4.2 million disabled people were employed, an increase from 2.9 million in 2013.[57] The employment rate gap between disabled men and disabled women has reduced, and the overall unemployment rate for disabled people has roughly halved between 2013 and 2019.

A note on intersectionality

One cannot get a complete picture of progress of DEI – or the lack thereof – without adopting an intersectional view. In her pivotal 1989 piece, Professor Kimberlé Crenshaw writes: 'Because the intersectional experience is greater than the sum of racism and sexism, any analysis that does not take intersectionality into account cannot sufficiently address the particular manner in which Black women are subordinated.'[58]

A 2023 study by Catalyst of 2,734 women from marginalised racial and ethnic groups across five countries found that: women with darker skin tones were more likely to experience discrimination compared to those with lighter skin tones; queer (63%) and transgender (67%) women are particularly likely to experience racism at work, compared with cisgender heterosexual women (49%); while 25% of the participants believed that senior leaders in their organisation would discriminate against an employee based on their ethnicity, race or culture in the form of overt and covert racism that included negative assumptions, belittling insults, disparaging remarks, discriminatory actions and outright racial slurs.[59]

Women with a visible disability (66%) and transgender women (64%) are more likely to be worried about non-inclusive behaviours than women who don't identify as being part of these groups. 40% of women belonging to an ethnic minority in their home country and 45% of women with a disability have experienced microaggressions at work, compared to 30% of women who are not from these groups. More than half of LGBTQ+ women have experienced microaggressions, compared to fewer than 3 in 10 women who are not LGBTQ+.[60] Nearly one in six (15%) women experiencing challenges relating to menstruation, menopause or fertility feel that speaking up about this at work would affect their career progression. Notably, 1 in 10 believes doing so would make them vulnerable to redundancy.[61]

Looking at the data, it is evident that progress has been limited and that to reach more equitable and inclusive workplaces, more must be done. Yet, growing backlash and resistance have us headed in the wrong direction. The number of companies without a DEI programme *increased* between 2020 and 2023[62] and there was an 18% average decrease in the number of leaders who endorsed their company's overall DEI efforts. According to the 2024 Global Human Capital Trends report by Deloitte,[63] there is a lot of talk but not enough action. While 76% of companies recognise the importance of human sustainability and DEI, only 10% are taking concrete steps to make progress happen. So, what is going on? Despite the compelling evidence that our workplaces are not equitable or inclusive, why are we seeing this backlash and resistance? Why are we not making more progress?

To answer these questions, we have to explore the backlash and resistance to DEI in greater depth.

Chapter 2

The backlash and resistance

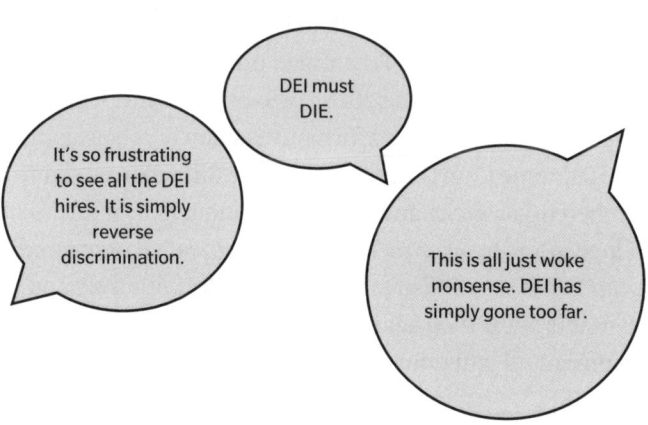

In December 2023, Elon Musk posted that 'DEI must DIE'.[64] Musk claimed that Diversity, Equity and Inclusion are 'propaganda words' that were acts of reverse discrimination and 'the point was to end discrimination, not replace it with different discrimination'.[65]

Musk's tweet was followed by Lululemon's founder, Chip Wilson, sharing his criticism of the company's DEI efforts, stating that the company is 'trying to become like the Gap, everything to everybody'. He referred to the people in Lululemon's ads as 'sickly' and 'unhealthy' and dismissed the diversity of sizes, ages, races, genders and styles as 'not inspirational'.[66]

And the headlines continued:

'Hamstrung by "golden handcuffs": Diversity roles disappear 3 years after George Floyd's murder inspired them'[67]

'DEI Progress is Facing a Concerning Reversal'[68]

'Corporate Diversity Pledges Fizzle Amid Layoffs'[69]

The tweets and headlines are all part of a series of incidents of societal, legislative and corporate backlash to DEI efforts. In 2024, nine states in the USA explicitly banned the use of affirmative action in employment processes following the 2023 US Supreme Court legislation that explicitly rejected race-based affirmative action in college admissions. After the Supreme Court ruling, billionaire Bill Ackman claimed that DEI is 'inherently a racist and illegal movement in its implementation even if it purports to work on behalf of the so-called oppressed'.[70] The ruling has led to scrutiny of private-sector DEI initiatives and a number of lawsuits being filed against companies for favouring women and underrepresented individuals.

In March 2024, in the aftermath of the collapse of the Francis Scott Key Bridge in Baltimore, social media posts appeared targeting Baltimore Mayor Brandon Scott. The posts referred to Scott, who is black, as a 'DEI mayor' – with DEI standing in for 'didn't earn it' – suggesting that Scott did not earn his high-level position. In March 2024, across the pond in the UK, the country's Minister of State for Women and Equalities, Kemi Badenoch, announced that DEI initiatives are ineffective and counterproductive, and 'have little to no tangible impact'.[71] A month later, Badenoch said, 'I'm a woman of colour. DEI is just woke indoctrination.'[72]

Earlier in the year, US company Boeing was facing its own challenge with DEI when an Alaska Airlines Boeing 737-9 Max aircraft experienced a midair blowout that left a gaping hole in the plane and forced an emergency landing in Portland, Oregon. What could DEI have to do with that? Well, insiders blamed DEI for the incident as well as recent safety concerns plaguing the company, citing that DEI was 'anti-excellence', ill-defined and created power-hungry executives who focused excessively on DEI at the expense of safety.[73] Similar comments arose during CrowdStrike's global IT outage with Elon Musk blaming diversity efforts for the outage.[74]

Then, in May 2024, the former president of the USA, Donald Trump, vowed to fight the 'anti-white feeling' in the USA if elected to office.[75] In July 2024, the democratic candidate for president of the USA in the country's elections, Kamala Harris, was referred to as a 'DEI hire' by a Republican, despite having held the following positions – vice-president of the USA, senator, attorney-general and district attorney.[76]

In August 2024, in response to conservative commentator Robby Starbuck, Harley Davidson dropped its DEI efforts.[77] This was the latest in a string of companies that included agricultural equipment maker Deere & Co. and farming goods retailer Tractor Supply Co. that have taken similar actions in response to his attacks. In a post on X, he wrote: 'We don't want you pushing political messages, social messages at work. I'm not asking you to become a conservative company. I'm asking you to be neutral. I'm asking you to make it a welcoming place for everybody, which means getting rid of DEI, getting rid of wokeness and just being a workplace again.'[78]

This backlash to DEI initiatives isn't just the case in the USA.

The past two decades have seen a steady rise in anti-immigration sentiment and xenophobia[79] across both Europe and the USA, propelled by far-right political parties. August 2024 saw widespread anti-immigration and anti-Muslim riots across the UK.[80] While these extreme views may be seen to arise from a desire to protect 'local' jobs and preserve 'local' culture, they are bad for business and the economy.[81] In early 2024, German CEOs raised concerns that the proposed anti-immigration policies of the far-right party AfD were harming the country's reputation as an attractive destination for foreign investment and skilled workers amid a shortage of domestic labour that is hampering growth.[82]

In Early 2024, the University of Auckland faced significant backlash for creating designated spaces for indigenous and marginalised Māori and Pacific students. ACT New Zealand, a right-wing political party, claimed the spaces were racist.[83] The country's deputy prime minister and New Zealand First leader, Winston Peters, claimed that the university's actions were comparable to racist groups such as the Ku Klux Klan. Despite the intense backlash, the university stood by its decision to provide safe spaces for minority groups.

Not far from New Zealand, in the same year, an Australian man launched legal proceedings, alleging that he was discriminated against because he did not have access to a specific exhibit at Tasmania's Museum of Old and New Art (MONA) with his entry ticket. The Ladies Lounge exhibit, by artist Kirsha Kaechele, was a women-only space, created to highlight the discrimination and exclusion many women have experienced through history. While the museum has been ordered to stop refusing entry to 'persons who do not identify as ladies', the exhibit certainly achieved its objective.[84]

DEI efforts face resistance from broader political and social narratives. From a ban on the hijab in sports competitions to abayas in schools in France to the nearly two anti-Muslim hate speech events per day in India, actions that foster anti-Muslim sentiments are on the rise.[85] In the 2024 Olympics, while it was the most gender-balanced Olympics to date, French athletes wearing head scarves were banned from competing in the prestigious global sporting competition.[86]

Similarly, political and social narratives have a significant influence on the backlash towards the transgender community. In 2023, the UK's prime minister, Rishi Sunak, made the statement: 'A man is a man, and a woman is a woman. That's just common sense,' during his speech at an annual conference of the Conservative Party. He is not alone in his views. Since 2019, *Harry Potter* author J.K. Rowling has been very vocal on social media and in articles about her views on gender identity, particularly not allowing transwomen into women-only spaces like toilets. A Home Office report in the UK said that comments like the ones made by Rowling and Sunak may have led to a rise in offences based on gender identity. In total, gender-based hate crimes have increased by 11%.[87] In May 2024, the cofounder and CEO of Olacabs.com made headlines when he posted the following on X: 'Most of us in India have no clue about politics of this pronoun illness. People do it because it's become expected in our corporate culture, especially MNCs. Better to send this illness back where it came from. Our culture has always had respect for all. No need for new pronouns.'[88]

What is particularly alarming is the ideology gap in young men and women – the future talent pool of our organisations. In countries on every continent – in the USA, UK, Germany and South Korea – we see evidence of young men adopting more conservative views while young women are adopting more liberal views.[89] This is a recent development. Since 2015, the gap between young men and women has expanded dramatically with no signs of narrowing, and can be attributed to the view that gender rights have 'gone too far', propagated by extreme misogynist influencers like Andrew Tate.[90]

Looking at the news headlines and data, you wouldn't be wrong to assume that 'anti-DEI' narratives are growing in popularity. You may also be tempted to dismiss these and say, 'these are just a few vocal voices that dominate our news feeds'. But here is the thing – these vocal voices have influence on how large groups of people think and feel about DEI efforts, and in turn what happens in our organisations. Afterall, Elon Musk has over 190 million followers on X![91]

So, how has this backlash and resistance filtered into our organisations?

The backlash and resistance at work

When one of the leading HR organisations in the world, the Society of Human Resource Management (SHRM), announced in July 2024 that it was no longer focusing on 'equity' in its DEI approach, and was moving to use 'I&D' rather than 'IE&D', it may be safe to assume that DEI is in crisis.[92] While what we have seen so far are examples of more visible forms of backlash and resistance, there is also evidence of more subtle resistance from employees and leaders in organisations that reflect what we see and hear in wider society.

A 2024 report by the Institute for Corporate Productivity (i4cp) showed that 24% of the survey's respondents said external critics like media, politicians and social media posed the biggest obstacles to DEI efforts.[93] At the same time, about 37% said that managers were the top challengers of DEI initiatives while another 34% said it was frontline workers. Interestingly, when it came to challenging DEI efforts, senior leadership and customers came in last at 22% and 19%, respectively.

Based on my experience working with global companies on their DEI efforts, I categorise the backlash and resistance to DEI in people into three broad categories – the deniers, the passive resistors and the active resistors.

The deniers are people who do not believe that DEI programmes and activities are needed because there are no problems to fix, and so they choose not to implement any. They are in denial. To recognise this form of backlash, look for statements like:

> 'DEI is not a problem in our organisation, everyone is already treated equally.'
>
> 'Shouldn't we just treat each other like human beings? I personally don't see colour.'
>
> 'I behave appropriately so DEI does not concern me.'

The passive resistors are people whose backlash and resistance to DEI is more subtle and perhaps the most challenging to spot. On the surface, passive resistors might ignore DEI efforts or may even appear supportive at times. They may show up for DEI events, and attend training sessions without too much of a fuss but these actions may be disingenuous or performative in nature.[94] They may be silent, or they may engage to a reasonable degree. However, their support for DEI stops there. There is hesitation or even avoidance when it comes to taking action to implement change in their decision-making processes when hiring or promoting employees or in their interactions with others. The hesitation and avoidance could also be because they have had negative past experiences with DEI initiatives and/or their company's DEI team, and may view DEI efforts as doing more harm than good.[95] They may share excuses for why they cannot implement DEI actions. These passive behaviours reflect a misalignment – those exhibiting passive behaviours seem like they are onboard with DEI but distance themselves from taking any action that might make a real impact.[96] They might engage in even more passive backlash when they see the active backlash around them, further retreating into inaction.

In their research in *'Research to diversity and inclusion change initiatives'*, Maria Velasco and Chris Sansone identified the following passive resistance behaviours:[97]

- Agreeing verbally but not following through.
- Failing to implement change.
- Procrastinating or dragging feet.
- Feigning ignorance.
- Withholding information, suggestions, help or support.
- Standing by and allowing the change to fail.

The active resistors exhibit backlash and resistance through visible actions to block and hinder DEI efforts. Like denial, it is often easier to spot active resistors. In the same research, Maria Velasco and Chris Sansone identified the following active resistance behaviours:[98]

- Undermining by questioning the purpose and need for the initiative.
- Blocking by openly expressing opposition.
- Fault finding by being critical of cost, or that DEI doesn't fit with the culture of the organisation.
- Intimidating/threatening by pushing back and framing with vehemence.

- Manipulating/distorting facts by making accusations of hiring and promoting those who are unqualified.
- Appealing to fear by not 'rocking the boat' or making others feel uncomfortable.

In April 2023, Budweiser's flagship low-calorie beverage, Bud Light, faced intense backlash in response to a social media promotion the company conducted with actress and TikTok personality Dylan Mulvaney, a transgender woman.[99] As a result of this backlash, the company took a severe hit. Bud Light's sales fell between 11 and 26%,[100] the company's stock price fell 20% and, by May of 2023, Bud Light lost its status as the top-selling beer in the United States – a spot it had held for 20 years.[101] In response to the consumer backlash, the company paused all influencer marketing until it had developed more robust procedures for vetting such collaborations.

In May 2023, social media posts called for a boycott of the US retailer Target in response to the store's Pride Month merchandise.[102] In response to the online outrage and threats against employees, Target removed several pieces of merchandise from its website as well as some stores in the southern USA. The company also decided to move its Pride displays in some locations from the entrance areas to the back of the store. To justify these changes, Target cited concern for the safety of its employees.

In June 2023, Danish Biotech company Chr Hansen responded to threats against the company's US employees, who experienced 'violent verbal aggression' from US customers and business partners, by removing the rainbow flag from the company's social media channels and communicating that they would no longer be a sponsor of the Copenhagen Pride event. This was seen as a significant withdrawal of their support for the LGBTQ+ community and resulted in over 400 employees writing a letter of protest. The employee letter emphasised that they saw the reversal as an action of the company putting profit and support for shareholders and customers above the working environment of their own employees.

At the top of the hierarchy, active resistance to DEI efforts are apparent through a lack of prioritisation of DEI efforts and an inadequate allocation of resources to support the agenda.[103] A Revelio Labs analysis showed that after reaching their peak in early 2023, DEI positions dropped by 5% by the end of 2023.[104] An analysis of over 500,000 C-suite hirings between 2019 and 2022 found that, after experiencing significant growth in 2020 and 2021,[105] chief diversity officer (CDO) hires declined in 2022. What is especially concerning is that CDOs were the only C-suite position to experience hiring declines in 2022.

It is not just DEI positions being axed. DEI programmes and Employee Resource Groups (ERGs) are also affected by the backlash. A Glassdoor survey revealed that access to Diversity, Equity and Inclusion (DEI) programmes increased to 39% in 2020 before peaking at 43% in 2021, before falling to 41% in 2022.[106] ERGs are grassroots, voluntary groups in organisations led by employees who share a characteristic – gender, ethnicity, religious affiliation, lifestyle or interest – whose purpose is to provide career development and personal support to create a safe space where employees can be themselves. Today, fewer companies are funding ERGS. In 2020, 78% of all ERGs received money from their host companies but, by 2023, that figure had dropped to 70%.[107]

Not wanting to seem like they are not supportive of DEI efforts, many organisations have used the excuse of weaker economic conditions to justify these cuts. This, of course, is counter to research that shows that companies that prioritise DEI through a recession are more resilient, build a positive brand image, address the shortage of workers and prevent alienating their customer base.[108] A survey in 2020 found that, during the Great Recession of 2007 to 2009, companies with inclusive workplaces (rated by historically marginalised groups) outperformed companies where employees lacked inclusivity by nearly four times in their stock performance.

Backlash and resistance from DEI practitioners, inclusive leaders and people from marginalised groups

While it may seem that the backlash and resistance comes from those who are from well-represented and majority groups, what about DEI practitioners and inclusive leaders who advocate for DEI? What about people who are part of marginalised groups? These are the people who are often the most invested in DEI efforts. Do they demonstrate any backlash and resistance? It turns out that they do. While there is little evidence to suggest a denial of DEI initiatives from these groups, we do see both passive and active backlash and resistance from these groups.

It may be hard to believe but even DEI practitioners and business leaders who advocate for DEI exhibit passive backlash and resistance behaviours, usually in response to the denial or active backlash that they witness around them. The backlash that is often directed at them can be so intense that it can push even the most dedicated DEI practitioner and advocate into avoidance – where they stop actively engaging to avoid getting 'burnt'. Despite its high status and compensation, the average tenure of those doing DEI work is just three years[109] and the main reason DEI practitioners give for leaving is that the work was emotionally taxing.[110] What about business leaders who are proponents of DEI? The vocal backlash to DEI has led to many senior leaders and CEOs, even those who have supported DEI efforts in the past, keeping silent and maintaining a low profile when it comes to DEI. In his 2024 shareholder letter, Jamie Dimon, CEO of JP Morgan Chase, talked about the bank's continued commitment to Diversity, Equity and Inclusion without actually using the term, DEI.[111]

For people who are part of marginalised groups, the passive backlash and resistance to DEI initiatives may occur due to a desire to avoid the perception of receiving 'special treatment' from the company, not wanting to be known only for their marginalised identity or not wanting to share their discrimination experiences at DEI events. Members of marginalised groups don't just exhibit passive backlash or resistance, however. Both The Great Resignation and quiet quitting are phenomena that reflect an active backlash to the lack of progress of current DEI efforts, with bias and discrimination continuing to be rampant in workplaces.

The Great Resignation refers to the 2021–2 trend in the USA, India, China, Australia and Europe of large numbers of employees voluntarily resigning from their jobs, with women leaving at a consistently higher rate than men.[112] Why? The main reasons discussed are low pay, limited opportunities for career advancement, hostile work environments, inflexible remote-work policies and long-lasting job dissatisfaction.[113] According to research published in *MIT Sloan Management Review*, a toxic work culture was the top predictor of this mass resignation. In fact, a toxic culture was 10.4 times more likely to contribute to attrition than compensation. The leading elements contributing to toxic cultures included failure to promote DEI, workers feeling disrespected and unethical behaviour.[114]

A 2023 DDI report titled 'The Great Diversity Departure' reveals that women and minority leaders at all levels are leaving organisations at higher numbers than their non-minority, male counterparts in the USA.[115] At junior levels, 33% of minority men plan to leave their current organisation to advance their career as they do not believe they can progress at their current company; this number increases to 41% for minority women and compares with 19% for non-minority men. At more senior levels, the trends remain similar with 46% of minority men planning to leave their current organisation to advance their career; with the number increasing to 49% for minority women compared to 29% for non-minority men. The report also highlights what is needed for leaders from diverse backgrounds to stay in the company: trust with senior leaders, opportunities for growth and development, leaders and managers who listen and respond with empathy and a company culture that is inclusive to different perspectives.

Another display of active backlash and resistance is quiet quitting. Quiet quitting is when employees remain in the company, but they mentally check out and do the minimum amount of work for their role without any extra commitment or passion, while also setting boundaries between the job and life outside the job.[116] Quiet quitting was first coined by the economist Mark Boldger in 2009. The term gained popularity in 2021 in China with the related concept of 'lying flat' and, in 2022, by Bryan Creely, a corporate recruiter turned coach. Gallup's 2023 'State of the Global Workplace' report concluded that 59% of the workers worldwide were 'quiet quitting'.[117] The main causes were issues with culture, pay and well-being. Coupled with the lack of recognition, these causes make employees feel undervalued or devalued.[118] This quiet quitting – left unaddressed – can lead to *conscious quitting*,[119] where employees actually leave their jobs, or *career cushioning*,[120] where employees start lining up a new gig while still working at their current one.

According to Dr Ella F. Washington, a DEI expert and professor at Georgetown University's McDonough School of Business, 'Quiet quitting is nothing new. Post-2020 people really took the time to evaluate what's important to them. For employees who weren't able to participate in the Great Resignation, quiet quitting is a way to combat the feeling that work is not giving them what they need.'[121] However, Dr Washington cautions that, while 49% of black employees want to quit,[122] it is harder for people of colour to resign or engage in quiet quitting due to the prevailing biases that may mean harsher consequences. Employees from marginalised groups become frustrated by the inability to be themselves in a workplace that was not created and built to be inclusive of their diverse needs. In such a toxic culture, these employees are more likely to feel pressured – in both overt and subtle ways – to conform to the dominant norms to survive in an environment where their voice isn't being heard and respected, resulting in further dissatisfaction and stress. For black employees who are considering or actively looking for a new job, pay transparency, alignment between their personal and company values and a diverse leadership team are the top drivers.[123]

Having looked at the evidence, it is safe to say that there is significant backlash and resistance to DEI. This backlash and resistance is limiting the progress and impact of DEI efforts which, in turn, leads to further backlash and resistance. And the vicious cycle continues. A key question on my mind was, why? Why are we experiencing this backlash and resistance in the very first place? Let's dig a little deeper.

Are you resistant to DEI?

Circle the response that best applies to you at the end of each statement. Be honest with yourself.

Can I say that:

- I feel that my organisation does not need DEI initiatives and that everything is going great. Yes/No/Maybe
- I think DEI initiatives are unnecessary, a waste of time and/or just another corporate initiative that will go away in a few months. Yes/No/Maybe
- I feel anxious that everything around me at work is changing rapidly. Yes/No/Maybe
- I said I would implement a DEI initiative and then procrastinated or found an excuse not to. Yes/No/Maybe
- I pretended that I didn't know what a DEI initiative was about to avoid engaging in it. Yes/No/Maybe
- I don't want to be perceived to be receiving any 'special treatment' from the company so I stay away from DEI initiatives. Yes/No/Maybe
- I don't want to be the spokesperson for all marginalised groups just because I am from one. Yes/No/Maybe
- I avoid engaging actively in DEI initiatives and conversations because of the backlash and resistance I see around me, even though I want to. Yes/No/Maybe
- I have withheld information, suggestions, help or support for DEI efforts. Yes/No/Maybe
- I have intentionally allowed a DEI initiative to fail. Yes/No/Maybe
- I have questioned and/or opposed the need for DEI initiatives. Yes/No/Maybe
- I identified evidence that DEI will 'rock the boat' and is not suited for my organisation. Yes/No/Maybe

➤

- I have tried to block DEI initiatives by withholding information or resources for such efforts. Yes/No/Maybe
- I have openly communicated that my organisation's DEI efforts have gone too far in hiring and promoting people who are unqualified. Yes/No/Maybe

- -

If you answered yes or maybe to any of the above statements, ask yourself if you may be the denier, the passive resistor or the active resistor. Pen down your thoughts in your notebook. If it feels uncomfortable to reflect on the reasons at this stage, come back to it later on after you have read more of the book. In Chapter 6, I explore this discomfort and offer tools to help us get comfortable with the discomfort. You may wish to come back to this exercise then. The first step to being more inclusive is to acknowledge that we are being resistant, and then exploring why.

Making sense of the backlash and resistance

You may be wondering, why are we seeing so much backlash and resistance to DEI? After all, so much has been written in academic research, as well as practitioner books and articles about the need for DEI. So much has been reported in the media about the inequity and inequality that exists. We have established a strong business, societal and human case for DEI. We have extensive research on what needs to be done. We have experts who have provided evidence-based strategies for nurturing inclusive and equitable workplaces. We see that DEI is a key part of the strategy of many organisations, with leaders hired to facilitate.

Yet, instead of leveraging the know-how to build on the progress so far, DEI efforts are being used as a scapegoat for everything from faulty aeroplanes to problems with our education and healthcare systems to the polarisation in society. In response, companies are cutting funding and shrinking DEI budgets, and downsizing DEI functions, preventing actual cultural and systemic change from happening.

Why are we here?

The answer to this lies in the fact that DEI efforts have excessively focused on the following:

- Affirmative action as a 'quick fix' without channelling resources and efforts to systemic and cultural change,

- The business case for DEI, rather than on the fairness and moral case,

- Simplistic solutions for a complex problem.

All or some combination of these reasons have led to the backlash and resistance we see, and the limited progress of DEI efforts.

The limitations of affirmative action

Affirmative action is defined as 'any measure, beyond simple termination of a discriminatory practice, adopted to correct or compensate for past or present discrimination or to prevent discrimination from recurring in the future'.[124] Affirmative action is often accompanied by quotas, which are targets that are set by organisations and teams to ensure that there is adequate representation of marginalised groups. These actions are undertaken in an effort to address systemic inequity.

Though well-intentioned, the challenges of affirmative action lie in the legal, moral and economic questions that arise from the preferential treatment of certain groups over others. Underlying the backlash to DEI are various concerns of reverse discrimination, or the unfair disadvantage to individuals who are from historically privileged backgrounds who benefit from the structures, systems and practices that favour them over others.[125] While affirmative action may increase the numbers of organisational members from underrepresented groups, there is the real risk that it is seen as tokenism or nothing more than a symbolic effort, masking actual progress. Over time, affirmative action does a disservice to underrepresented groups by perpetuating the bias that the person 'didn't earn' a position or place through their skills, competencies and behaviours, but only through advantage. Affirmative action does not address the systemic and cultural bias that often results in people from underrepresented backgrounds and identities being overlooked. The assumption that the people who have been hired in the past have been deserving of the role is the myth of meritocracy. We want to believe that people are 'chosen and moved into positions of success, power, and influence on the basis of their demonstrated abilities and merit'.[126] This is far from reality. When we hold this assumption, affirmative action can cause resentment among historically well-represented groups who see those being given opportunities as not being worthy.

One consequence of affirmative action is that DEI is seen as a zero-sum game where one group 'wins' at the expense of another group. This creates divisiveness, claims of reverse discrimination and the notion that 'DEI has gone too far'. DEI is the practice of giving all workers equal access to opportunities for employment, development and career advancement. DEI is not a pie, meaning that, once we give a piece to someone, there is less for others. This attitude, an unfortunate side-effect of affirmative action, misrepresents the intention and impact of DEI efforts. When DEI efforts are done right – addressing the systemic and cultural bias at play – there is space for everyone.

Affirmative action is often seen as a 'quick fix' by leaders hoping that simply hiring people from underrepresented groups will solve the root causes. This false assumption has led to years of limited support with a lack of prioritisation and accountability by leadership. This lack of support often results in insufficient resources directed towards DEI strategy development and initiatives that would work to raise awareness, address the systemic and cultural biases and build robust metrics to assess progress.

What we see happening in the USA with backlash to affirmative action should act as a cautionary tale to the EU where new legislation coming into effect in 2026 will require large companies operating in the region to ensure a share of 40% of the 'underrepresented sex' – usually women – among non-executive directors. Without addressing the root causes of systemic and cultural bias, when affirmative action is ended, any prior progress made is likely to be reversed. We see this in the higher education sector in the USA. Following the 2023 Supreme Court decision to end affirmative action, the Massachusetts Institute of Technology (MIT) reported in August 2024 that only 16% of its new intake identified as being black, Hispanic, Native American and/or

Pacific Islander. This was down 10 percentage points in just one year. Both the dean of admissions and president of MIT made statements that the university would have left out many well-qualified, well-matched applicants, and that the MIT community was not as racially and ethnically diverse as it had been previously.[127]

While the backlash to affirmative action is concerning, I am beginning to see companies pivot their emphasis away from the quotas/targets they had set to making the systemic and cultural change necessary to make their workplaces fairer and more equitable. In my work with global companies, I am seeing greater efforts being made to ensure that hiring and talent development processes, as well as pay scales, are more equitable and fair. This is, perhaps, an unintentional positive outcome of the open backlash and legislative changes to affirmative action in the USA.

The limitations of the business case

Plenty has been written about the business case to DEI, from improved financial returns as a result of better decision making and greater innovation, to improved productivity and job satisfaction and capturing new markets as a result of better understanding of customer needs. Research done by Oriane Georgeac and Aneeta Rattan shows that 80% of Fortune 500 companies used the business case to justify the importance of diversity, while less than 5% used the fairness case – the case that DEI efforts should be the result of a moral understanding that fairness is right; that DEI efforts are the right thing to do.[128] For the groups that DEI is supposed to support, grounding DEI efforts in the business case results in some unfortunate outcomes. In their research, underrepresented participants who read a business case for diversity anticipated feeling 11% less of a sense of belonging, were 16% more concerned that they would be stereotyped and were 10% more concerned that the company would view them as interchangeable with other members of their identity group. This is in comparison to those who read a fairness case. Compared to those who read neutral messaging, participants who read a business case reported being 27% more concerned about stereotyping and lack of belonging, and they were 21% more concerned they would be seen as interchangeable. When a company made a business case, the participants' perceptions that its commitment to diversity was genuine fell by up to 6%, making the underrepresented participants less interested in working for the organisation. Based on these findings, the authors wonder why, if most organisations don't feel the need to explain why they care about core values such as innovation, resilience or integrity, they feel compelled to justify the need for diversity?

Looking ahead, I hope that organisations adopt a social justice angle to DEI, using their size and clout to actively shape society and address the injustice and inequity in the world.

The limitations of simplification

In many of the conversations I have had about the backlash to DEI, there is a common viewpoint that we need to simplify DEI to make it work. The DEI leaders I have engaged with say that their business leaders are busy and have multiple priorities, so DEI needs to be made 'simple and easy'. But what is 'simple and easy' a code for? Could it be that we want DEI initiatives to be 'comfortable' for business leaders who, more often than not, belong to dominant and well-represented groups?

I struggle with the idea of simplification. After all, the way we have approached DEI until now is a simplified approach, and it is this desire for simplification that has resulted in:

• Quotas and targets focusing on a very narrow view of diversity with all its challenges and 'side effects',

• Quick fix and performative efforts that provide superficial and short-term change, but look good on the annual report,

• 'Fix-the-minority' initiatives that are 'easier', cheaper and don't require leaders from well-represented identities to change how they lead.

None of the above addresses the systemic and cultural root causes. So, given where we are and the slow progress we are making, I don't believe simplification is what is needed. Addressing systemic and interpersonal bias, and nurturing inclusion is not easy. It is complex and intersectional, requiring multiple systems to change. Cultural transformation requires mindset and behaviour shifts, together with broader systemic change. DEI requires change at all levels – individual, team, function, organisational, institutional and societal. It requires us to change our own ways of thinking, how we see others and interact, and how we make decisions. This is not simple. It is complex. And it is uncomfortable. In my leadership workshops, if I have not made you uncomfortable, then I have not done my job.

We have to get comfortable with the discomfort that comes with DEI initiatives.

Human beings and our environments are complex. Until we embrace complexity and intersectionality, our progress in nurturing inclusive, diverse and equitable workplaces will continue to remain limited. Instead of simplification, what if we provided leaders with greater clarification and guidance to lead inclusively through the complexity? What if we focused on the progress of our employees from diverse backgrounds feeling included, and not on perfection in achieving a target of representation? Embracing this complexity requires us to engage in consistent effort and a long-term vision, demonstrate a commitment to address the systemic and cultural issues and ensure sufficient resourcing of the efforts to enable systemic change to happen. Leaders who lean into the complexity and are willing to get uncomfortable are leaders who lead inclusively.

Going deeper

Unfortunately, today, DEI has become a polarising weapon often used for political gain. It has become politicised. In using it as such, politicians and leaders of organisations opposing DEI efforts are communicating that they are anti-fairness; that they want an organisation and society where some people have unfair advantages over others. Why? Because it serves themselves, others like them and their agenda well. While it may be easy to say no to the acronym DEI, not many people will say no to uniqueness, fairness and belonging. It is easy to say that they are anti-DEI or anti-woke, and that 'DEI must DIE',[129] but I do wonder how many of them would be comfortable to openly say, 'Fairness must DIE'?

The backlash and resistance to DEI in our workplaces is experienced by those who are part of dominant groups as well as those who are part of marginalised groups. It can take the form of outright denial of the need for DEI, passive backlash and resistance that includes avoidance or hesitation towards engaging actively in DEI change initiatives, and more active overt backlash or resistance to DEI. Understanding this backlash is what I've spent the past two years researching. I've been curious to explore why this backlash and resistance – whether it is more overt or subtle – exists in the first place and what is causing it.

So far, I have provided a set of explanations for the limited progress made and, to some extent, the backlash and resistance, but those do not go deep enough to the core reasons for the backlash and resistance we are seeing and experiencing. To break the vicious cycle of backlash and resistance, and limited progress, we must dig deeper. The explanations so far don't answer the following questions: Why are we not making progress with systemic and cultural change? Why are we not grounding DEI in the fairness case? Why are we seeking simplification for something that is complex?

To answer these questions, I draw on the body of research that focuses on making sense of the resistance to DEI in organisations. The research focuses on understanding why people resist social change, and show that DEI initiatives elicit *threat* in both those who are part of the dominant/well-represented groups[130] as well as DEI practitioners and inclusive leaders who advocate for DEI and employees from marginalised groups.[131] Based on this prior work, Table 2.1 provides a list of threats posed by DEI.

Table 2.1 Threats posed by DEI

Name of threat	Description of threat
Symbolic threat Threat to one's group's culture, values or beliefs	Occurs when people view DEI efforts as changing the very culture, values and beliefs of the organisation by recruiting, retaining and promoting people with beliefs different from their own.[132] Also occurs when people from marginalised groups view the backlash to DEI as changing the very culture, values and beliefs of the organisation away from inclusion and fairness

Name of threat	Description of threat
Status threat Threat to one's group or individual societal status	Refers to the threat experienced by those who are part of well-represented groups who feel that their status or resources are threatened. They perceive diversity initiatives as a zero-sum game and assume that if members of underrepresented groups make any gains – in opportunities, hires, the potential for promotion – those who are from well-represented groups like themselves would, in turn, incur losses. This can also occur when people from marginalised groups, DEI practitioners and inclusive leaders are negatively labelled as 'DEI/woke-police' because of their involvement in DEI work, resulting in them losing their status in the organisation. This may mean that DEI practitioners and inclusive leaders may avoid engaging in DEI initiatives to avoid getting 'burnt' by the backlash
Realistic threat Threat to one's group's resources (e.g. jobs, opportunities, etc.)	DEI efforts to recruit, retain and promote members of marginalised groups at higher rates (including affirmative action) are perceived by dominant group members as changes that threaten their own job security, as well as pay and promotion opportunities fuelling backlash.[133] On the other hand, people from marginalised groups, DEI practitioners and inclusive leaders may perceive their involvement in DEI efforts as non-promotable or career-limiting tasks hindering career progression or involvement in strategic decision making. They may view the backlash and resistance as a sign of limited progress, and then take actions that centre the comfort of those in dominant groups to avoid further conflict and backlash

➤

Table 2.1 continued

Name of threat	Description of threat
Existential threat Threat to one's group's existence	In political climates where people of the dominant group have been mobilised around their group's perceived existential threat with changing demographics and growing diversity, organisations may experience backlash, reflecting a concern of the changes occurring with marginalised group members replacing employees from the dominant group.[134] At the same time, with the severe backlash, people from marginalised groups can feel a threat to their existence in the organisation. Similarly, DEI practitioners can feel a threat to their existence with the roll back on roles and funding
Prototypicality threat Threat that one's subgroup will no longer be the quintessential representative of a group	Occurs when, for example, men who believed that men represented the prototypical membership of the STEM industry show more resistance towards DEI efforts to increase women's representation in STEM. Or white people feeling concerned by their declining share of the US population that threatens their status as the most prototypical ethnic group in the USA[135]
Meritocratic threat Threat that one's accomplishments are not due to personal merit	Occurs when people from dominant groups perceive that DEI initiatives imply that their achievements are not the result of their skills and qualities but rather because of their group membership.[136] They express discomfort that recognising the existence of bias, discrimination and inequality somehow 'explains away' their own successes. This form of threat is especially common among dominant group members who place value on systems that reward hard work and individual merit. Also occurs when people from marginalised groups are perceived as a 'token/diversity hire' receiving 'special treatment' from the company rather than being recognised for their accomplishments

Name of threat	Description of threat
Moral threat Threat to one's group being seen as 'bad'	Refers to the view that, by acknowledging privilege or unearned advantages, it tarnishes the moral image of those who are privileged by linking them to an unfair system. As human beings, we like to see ourselves as good people who are committed to equality. When this is shaken through DEI efforts, people feel threatened and uncomfortable
Exclusion threat Threat that DEI efforts exclude one's own group	People who are part of well-represented and dominant groups perceive DEI activities (for example, Employee Resource Groups) that focus on marginalised identities as being exclusionary. They may also feel that the language and vocabulary including acronyms and jargon being used in DEI activities are unfamiliar to them, making them feel excluded from conversations

Looking at these threats posed by DEI, it is clear that, within our organisations, many of us experience some form of threat from DEI initiatives and its backlash – whether we are part of the dominant groups, those who are marginalised and/or those who advocate for DEI.

According to neuroscience, when human beings experience a perceived threat, it triggers *fear*. If DEI initiatives are perceived as a threat, we can then deduce that, in turn, this threat triggers fear. In their paper, '*Resistance to diversity and inclusion change initiatives*', Maria Velasco and Chris Sansone present fear as an underlying source of resistance.[137] According to them, fear manifests as resistance. 'Employees oppose change out of fear of the unknown, uncertainty and failure to be considered or informed, generating perceptions of potential loss or instability.'[138] Feelings of fear grow stronger when people perceive that they might lose their privilege and power related to their job, position, income, power, authority and economic insecurity.[139] Through interviews with leaders, Velasco and Sansone identified three types of fear to change arising from DEI initiatives: fear of the unknown, fear of losing privilege and power; and fear of being excluded.[140] Over many years of working with global companies in the corporate and humanitarian sectors, I recognise this fear of DEI and I believe that, until we address this fear, we will continue to make limited progress.

You may be wondering – of all the core emotions of anger, fear, sadness, disgust, surprise, anticipation, trust and joy[141] – why fear? Why not anger, for example? Surely there must be anger at play in the backlash and resistance. While fear and anger have many similarities, fear is often the trigger of anger.[142] To make progress, we need to peel back the backlash and dig deeper. This desire to understand the root causes of the backlash, resistance and limited progress is what prompted me to focus on fear by seeking answers to the following questions:

- What evidence can we find to support prior research on there being a fear of DEI?
- Who is fearful of DEI and what are people fearful of?
- How do we let go of this fear to embrace DEI efforts?

Let's begin with taking a deeper look into fear.

Chapter 3

What is fear?

I just don't know what to do. I feel so helpless.

DEI initiatives make me nervous and uneasy. Are my job and future opportunities being threatened?

DEI means that so much has to change. I feel overwhelmed and anxious by the sheer scale of change that is needed.

According to neuroscience, when human beings experience a perceived threat, it triggers the emotion *fear* in the part of the brain called the amygdala. Fear is a natural human emotion – experienced by everyone – that helps us detect and respond to real or perceived danger. In their book, *Rewire Your Anxious Brain*, Catherine Pittman and Elizabeth Karle write that fear is 'typically associated with a clear, present and identifiable threat' and, in this book, the perceived threat is DEI initiatives.

Though fear can often feel unpleasant, as an emotion it is part of our human experience. In fact, some fears can serve us well and are in place to protect us. Fear can motivate us to take action to secure or safeguard ourselves and to stay focused and alert. At the same time, there are other fears that do not serve us well. These fears can be debilitating, preventing us from trying new things and moving out of our comfort zone.

The research on emotions has evolved. During the 1970s, psychologist Paul Eckman identified six basic emotions that he suggested were universally experienced in all human cultures: happiness, sadness, disgust, fear, surprise and anger. He later expanded his list to include such things as pride, shame, embarrassment and excitement.[143] Psychologist Robert Plutchik uses a 'wheel of emotions'[144] to illustrate the theory that basic emotions act like building blocks for more complex emotions. More recent research includes 27 distinct categories of interconnected emotions, one of which is fear.[145] It is safe to say that fear is a core human emotion.

When we think of fear, we may think primarily of panic and extreme anxiety when, in fact, there is a range of different emotions associated with fear. Everything from feeling helpless, overwhelmed, worried or inadequate, to feeling excluded, persecuted, nervous and exposed.[146] Drawing on prior research that explores emotions, Figure 3.1 shows the emotions associated with fear. In this book, this is the breadth of expressions of fear I adopt when looking at the fear of DEI.

In looking at fear as comprising these various emotions, it is likely that we have all experienced fear at some point. When we were young, we may have felt nervous to get on a swing at the playground, or anxious when entering a new classroom at the start of the school year. We may

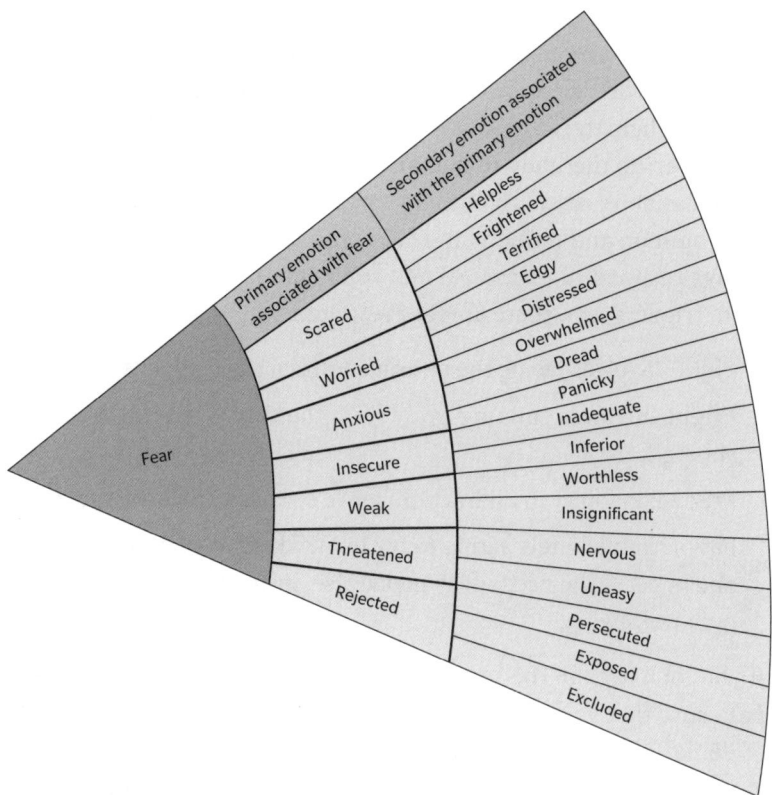

Figure 3.1 Emotions associated with the Fear of DEI

have been frightened when walking down a dark alley, or worried when interviewing for a job. We may have experienced feeling overwhelmed when making a pitch, or inadequate when presenting to the board. This entire spectrum of emotions is rooted in fear.

Fear reactions

You have probably heard the phrase 'fight or flight'. The concept of fight or flight as a stress response was created by US physiologist Walter Cannon in his 1915 book, *Bodily Changes in Pain, Hunger, Fear and Rage*.[147] His research was based on his studies of what happened when a predator threatened an animal. He found that the animal being threatened released the hormones epinephrine and adrenaline, which triggered the fight or flight response. Cannon highlighted that this process happened unconsciously and automatically and served to help the animal defend itself in life-threatening situations by preparing the body to run away or stay and fight. In the years since Cannon's research, numerous psychologists and physiologists have built on and refined Cannon's work to understand how human beings respond to threats. When confronted with a threat that, in turn, triggers fear, there are four responses:[148]

Fight: involves facing the perceived threat aggressively.

Flight: involves running away from the threat to protect or save yourself.

Freeze: inability to take action, move or speak against a threat.

Fawn: immediately acting to try to avoid any conflict or to please and appease the needs of someone else, instead of prioritising their own well-being.

If you look back to the section on backlash in the previous chapter, I am sure that you can recognise all these reactions in the evidence of denial, passive and active backlash that we have explored so far. We see companies who fight against DEI initiatives by withdrawing support for DEI roles and activities. We observe team leads retreat from discussions on DEI topics that make them feel uncomfortable. We notice employees who freeze, unable to take action when they witness or experience bias and discrimination from colleagues. We find DEI experts hesitating to pressure their resistant leaders to take action to avoid being in conflict with their colleagues.

Fear of fear

The word *fear* itself is something people are fearful of. In doing this research, I've been asked by business leaders and DEI experts about using the word fear – why explore something so negative? Why not adopt a more positive approach?

What I noticed was a fear of acknowledging that fear of DEI exists. While we may be willing to acknowledge that we are scared of flying on an aircraft or that we are fearful of dogs, openly acknowledging that we have a fear of inclusion, of people who are different and of fairness does not often sit well with our internal moral compass. This internal dissonance creates even more discomfort, stress and further resistance towards DEI. Why do we humans struggle with the emotion of fear? Why does fear make us feel so uncomfortable?

Fear is the elephant in the room we don't want to talk about, and I want to put fear on the table. But, why?

According to a psychologist I spoke to when doing this research, 'Fear is an emotion that we are trying to avoid. We see it as something that is dangerous to us, shaking our sense of normality or sense of security. But we are not done with the work until we face fear.'

At work, we are hired to know what to do based on our skills, past experiences and competencies. We are rewarded for knowing. We expect the leaders in our organisations to be in control and to know what to do. In turn, they expect their employees to have specialised skills and competencies to execute what is needed. In this results-driven environment, there is no room for fear – for being worried, anxious or concerned. Or for being vulnerable to express these emotions openly. Even though fear is a fundamental human emotion, fear is often seen as a sign of weakness, of inadequacy and not being in control in our workplaces. These are not the signs we want to project at work. We don't want people to know that we are fearful and vulnerable. It's something that we try very hard to hide. Why? Because there is a chance that we may be punished rather than rewarded for being vulnerable and expressing our fears. This has resulted in employees focusing on positive emotions while suppressing negative emotions like fear in the workplace.[149] This toxic positivity breeds feelings of shame, guilt, sadness and anxiety,[150] and can lead to stress and burnout. But toxic positivity is denial[151] – denial of the real issues at play that need to be addressed.

For us to move the needle when it comes to DEI and address the backlash and resistance that exists, we have to understand the cause of the resistance – the fear of DEI. What are people fearful of when it comes to DEI? Once we know the fears people have of DEI, then we can become aware of it and let it go.

Fear of DEI: the evidence

In my research, I adopted a multimethod approach to finding evidence that would help develop a deeper understanding into fear of DEI, and answer the questions shared at the end of Chapter 2. The three data sets included a discourse analysis of global news articles over the period from 2023–4, survey data from a survey conducted in the first quarter of 2024, and qualitative interview data with 28 global DEI experts and practitioners, business leaders and psychologists in early 2024. The findings from these data sets, combined with prior research and my own experience working actively with global organisations over the past five years, form the basis of this book. In this section, I share the key findings from the data for those interested in the research. As mentioned in the author's note, if you enjoy knowing about the research behind this book, then this is the section for you. If not, a quick skim of this section may suffice.

What does the news tell us?

In seeking answers to the questions shared at the end of Chapter 2, I spent time in collaboration with my research assistant and Master's student at the Copenhagen Business School, Kirstine Pinderup Frandsen, conducting a discourse analysis of news articles from well-reputed and well-recognised news channels from different regions of the world to find out if there was evidence of fear in the popular discourse on resistance to DEI. We were keen to understand whether fear was present in different parts of the world, and if there were any differences in how anti-DEI sentiments showed up in the discourse across countries or regions.

Most of the articles were from the time period of February 2023 to April 2024, with about 9% of the articles dating further back to 2016–22, and were from the following news outlets: *New York Times*, *Forbes*, CNN, Fox News, Bloomberg, *The Guardian*, BBC, *The Telegraph*, *The Indian Express*, *Times of India*, Al Jazeera, *The Africa Report*, *Global Times*, Nikkei Asia, *South China Morning Post*, *Shanghai Daily*, *The Korean Times* and *The Australian* among others.

Out of the 210 news articles read, 56 were selected for coding, based on their relevance in looking at the topic of anti-DEI backlash and resistance. The vast majority (64%) of coded articles were from the USA and UK. The remaining articles were from East Asia (18%), India (11%) and Middle East & Africa (7%).

The articles were obtained through a keyword search using the following words: diversity, equity, inclusion, DEI, representation, affirmative action, fear and inclusivity. This initial search resulted in articles primarily in the USA and UK contexts. To broaden the search to other regions, the following words were used: fairness, equal opportunity, social justice, pay equity, belonging, accessibility, collaboration, empowerment, women, minority, ethnicity, LGBTQ+ and tokenism. This showed us that terminology on DEI is well understood and reflected in the news in the USA and UK contexts, and less so in other contexts. It is also worth noting that the recent backlash and resistance to DEI in the USA and UK is in opposition to DEI initiatives that were implemented after George Floyd's murder, whereas the anti-DEI, and particularly anti-LGBTQ+, sentiments in other regions have been there for much longer and are grounded in conservative societal beliefs.

The articles were then coded according to fear-associated emotions explored earlier in this chapter. It should be noted that each of the emotions associated with fear do not exist in silos; they overlap with other fear-associated emotions. We selected the category the evidence was best suited for given the context and tone of the article. Table 3.1 shows some of the evidence from the news articles to give you a flavour of the data.

In analysing the content of the news articles, here are some key themes that stood out:

Feelings of being worried, edgy, distressed, threatened, nervous and uneasy were the predominant emotions, primarily revolving around the direct and indirect threat of DEI initiatives.

The nature of the threat varied, ranging from DEI being perceived as reverse racism, threatening traditional family structures,

Table 3.1 Evidence of emotions associated with fear in news articles

Emotions associated with fear	Evidence of the emotion
Scared (helpless, frightened, terrified)	'Some senior leaders don't make the time to address DEI because they're so afraid of doing it wrong.' 'The right has villainised DEI from Disney World to Harvard University as an engine of left-wing indoctrination and the banks don't want to become a target for lawsuits claiming reverse discrimination.' 'Pandering to white voters who see expanded options for minorities as a personal threat, some state legislatures have recast diversity, equity and inclusion as dangers to the values, history and future of the nation.'
Worried (edgy, distressed)	'And what must inevitably follow when ability, performance and practical outcomes are downgraded in favour of a political ideology can only be toxic.' 'In the name of D.E.I, all too many institutions have violated their constitutional commitments to free speech, due process and equal protection of the law.' 'The agency charged with overseeing airlines, plane makers, airports and every other aspect of civil aviation in America has undertaken a diversity push meant to bring in workers whose inborn limitations make them plainly unsuitable for high-stakes, high-pressure roles.'

Emotions associated with fear	Evidence of the emotion
Anxious (overwhelmed, dread, panicky)	'You read that right: The severely intellectually disabled and the psychiatrically disabled (that's a euphemism for crazy) will now be involved in making sure that planes don't hit the ground or each other.' 'After explaining my predicament, the doctor asked if I was gay. I answered in the affirmative and he told me that they do not treat "evil people".' 'The fear of losing power or sharing leadership with women and individuals from diverse backgrounds can further exacerbate resistance to DEI efforts.'
Insecure (inadequate, inferior)	'In our experience, that fear of saying or doing the wrong thing, particularly in a way that exposes a company or its leaders to social opprobrium, has kept many organizations and leaders from meaningfully moving forward.' 'Bankers and lawyers contend they have little choice but to reframe or pause new diversity initiatives and to get ahead of the blowback and potential litigation.' 'As the pressure and threat of litigation mounted, executives began to revisit and scale back some of their most ambitious goals.'
Weak (worthless, insignificant)	'When I got the phone call to say I had got the job, we immediately spoke about the salary,' says Erin, who lives in Yorkshire, UK. 'I asked if the fact that I was earning more was going to make him feel bad. He said that yes, he likes it when he can do things for me that I can't afford to do, because it makes him feel like he's taking care of me.'

Table 3.1 continued

Emotions associated with fear	Evidence of the emotion
Threatened (nervous, uneasy)	'DEI Efforts Seen as a Threat to Men's Professional Identities.' 'There have been other hints from the authorities that the LGBTQ community could be a threat to social stability.' 'Erecting a barrier to the penetration of Western anti-family ideology.' 'Companies that had been bragging about their diversity, equity and inclusion progress in the three years since George Floyd's murder are now questioning whether they've set themselves up for future legal action.'
Rejected (persecuted, exposed, excluded)	'Replaced basic ideas of good and evil with a new rubric: the powerless (good) and the powerful (bad) . . . People were to be given authority in this new order not in recognition of their gifts, hard work, accomplishments, or contributions to society, but in inverse proportion to the disadvantages their group had suffered, as defined by radical ideologues.' '"We will dry the roots of sneaky acts aiming to destroy our family institution by supporting perverse political, social and individual trends," he told tens of thousands of flag-waving and chanting supporters.' 'Promoters of the transgender bills say they protect children from misguided parents and doctors, even though major medical associations endorse gender-affirming care as often necessary and sometimes life-saving.'

contradicting religious beliefs, being anti-constitutional, imposing Western ideology on Eastern nations, to posing a general threat to the nation. The specific worries or fear appear to be related to national contexts, with patterns observed such as the following:

- Concerns about anti-constitutionalism and reverse racism are prevalent in the US.
- Threats to traditional family structures are highlighted in the US, East Asia and Africa.
- The perceived threat to the nation's identity is emphasised in India, East Asia and the USA.

Emotions such as insecure, inadequate, inferior, weak, worthless and insignificant were underrepresented, likely because these feelings are expressed through other fear expressions.

The fear categories of insecure, inadequate, inferior, weak, worthless and insignificant are notably absent across articles, with only four instances when they occurred across all the articles. However, it is very likely that expressions of fear in these categories are encompassed in the emotions of feeling threatened, nervous and uneasy. Feelings of being threatened imply that there is some degree of insecurity, inadequacy or weakness. Also, many fear expressions stem from statements made by DEI opponents who may not explicitly convey feelings of insecurity or weakness but express them through other fear expressions.

Anti-DEI discussions in US and East Asian media are characterised by a war discourse.

In reviewing the vocabulary use, we noticed the use of words and phrases such as 'under attack', 'our side is getting murdered', 'no agreed-on name for the enemy', 'threat to the future of America', 'propagandise our children', 'terrorism', 'authoritarian' and 'war on "woke capitalism"'.

African media does not extensively discuss DEI and is focused on increasing women's participation.

There is a notable absence of mentions of DEI or similar topics in African media, suggesting a lack of emphasis on DEI efforts beyond gender diversity in business. Additionally, African media exhibits strong anti-LGBTQ+ sentiment, with religion playing a role and LGBTQ+ individuals perceived as a threat to traditional family structures.

Anti-DEI sentiments in US media often revolve around the belief that DEI initiatives contradict the constitution and US values, particularly regarding equality under the law.

This sentiment is expressed through feelings of being worried, edgy, distressed, threatened, nervous, uneasy, in combination with a high prevalence of the emotions persecuted, rejected, nervous, and is exposed through the narratives of reverse racism. There appears to be a significant rise in fear after the Supreme Court ruled against affirmative action in June 2023. That has sparked fear of DEI across companies that are yet to adopt DEI initiatives as well as in companies that have previously been promoting diversity and inclusion. This fear is the fear of facing legal sanctions for existing or future DEI efforts.

From this discourse analysis, it is fairly clear that fear of DEI is present and reflected in mainstream media in many parts of the world. But how do people feel? Do they experience fear when engaging with DEI efforts? What are people fearful of and how do we let go of this fear to embrace DEI efforts?

What do people feel?

To understand how people feel about DEI and to dig deeper, I conducted a survey in the first quarter of 2024 to understand more general sentiments about DEI from a broader part of the population. An open call to complete the survey was shared through my LinkedIn network.

Demographic data

- 460 valid responses were collected out of 508 total responses.
- Respondents were from Asia & Middle East, Africa, Europe and North America.
- 97% of respondents were employees, managers and/or leaders.
- 34% of respondents worked in large multinational companies; 26% worked in small-to-medium-sized enterprises; 14% worked in a start-up/scale-up.
- 67% of respondents did not work in HR/talent management.
- 72% of respondents said that they were actively engaged in making their workplaces inclusive and equitable for diverse talent.

The key data points from the survey results (Figures 3.2 to 3.5) revealed that, while people may not see themselves as being resistant to DEI efforts, they witness resistance to these efforts at work. There

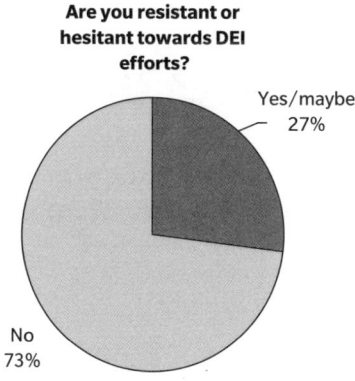

Are you resistant or hesitant towards DEI efforts?

Yes/maybe 27%

No 73%

Figure 3.2 Percentage of people resistant or hesitant towards DEI efforts

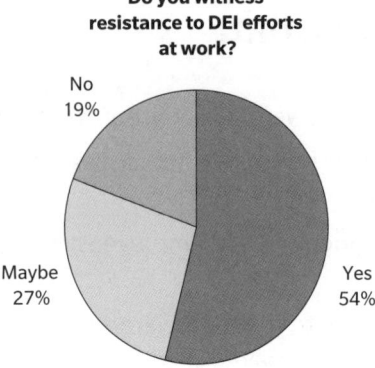

Figure 3.3 Percentage of people who witness resistance towards DEI efforts at work

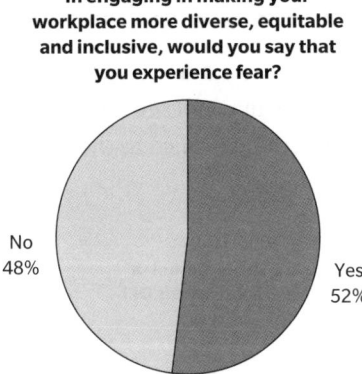

Figure 3.4 Percentage of people who experience fear in engaging in making their workplace more diverse, equitable and inclusive

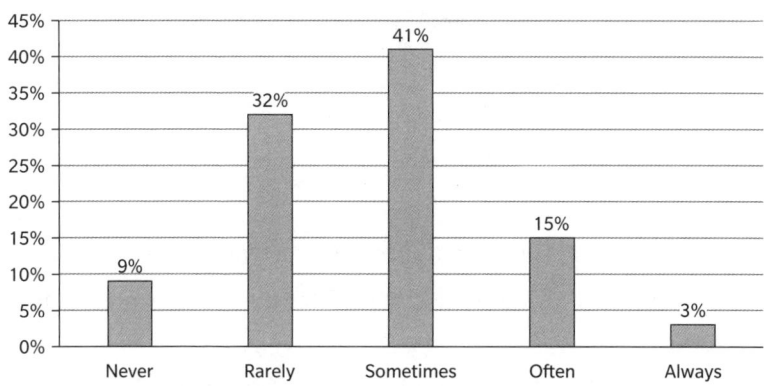

How frequently would you say that you experience fear?

Figure 3.5 Frequency with which people experience fear of DEI efforts

were slightly more respondents who experienced fear when engaging in making their workplaces more diverse, equitable and inclusive than those who did not. What was noteworthy was that 59% of respondents said that they experience fear sometimes, often or always.

The respondents also ranked their top 10 fears:

1 Fear of not knowing the right words and phrases.

2 Fear of failure or saying/doing the wrong thing.

3 Fear of being in situations of conflict with your colleagues when you address inequity, bias and discrimination that you witness or experience.

4 Fear of the impact of being seen as the 'DEI/woke police'.

5 Fear of not knowing enough about the DEI topic.

6 Fear of addressing the inequity, bias and discrimination that you witness or experience.

7 Fear of the impact of addressing bias on your career.

8 Fear of the impact of addressing bias on how others perceive you.

9 Fear of the discomfort of addressing your own bias; fear of the discomfort of needing to discuss difficult topics about DEI (e.g. inequity, bias and discrimination) with others (these were tied in ninth place).

10 Fear of being cancelled.

The top 5 actions that people believed would help them let go of their fear:

1 Knowing how to address bias in a constructive way.

2 Knowing how to be engaged in difficult and uncomfortable conversations.

3 An organisational and team culture where addressing inequity, bias and discrimination is valued and where I feel safe to address them.

4 Knowing when and how to stand up for someone else who is experiencing inequity, bias and discrimination.

5 Having greater know-how about DEI terms, words and phrases; knowing how to be comfortable with the uncomfortable moments; knowing how to deal with conflict well so it does not take a toll on your mental, emotional and physical well-being; knowing what to say and do in situations where there is inequity, bias and discrimination present (these were all tied in fifth place).

Now that we have firmly established that fear is at play, let's dig deeper.

What do the DEI professionals say?

To get a deeper understanding of fear of DEI and to seek answers to the questions posed at the end of Chapter 2, I spoke to 28 DEI professionals over a two-month period in early 2024. They included DEI experts and practitioners, business leaders who worked actively with DEI initiatives and psychologists who engage specifically on DEI-related issues. The interviewees' intersectional identities covered a wide range of visible and invisible dimensions of diversity. These experts had diverse expertise and experiences across global organisational contexts and industries.

With each of them, I set out to explore the following broad questions, hoping to leverage and learn from their wealth of experience working on DEI with companies, leaders and teams:

1 Would you say that fear is holding us back from making progress in the area of DEI in workplaces?
2 What are people fearful of when it comes to DEI?
3 What are you personally fearful of in working with DEI?

From the qualitative data collected, I worked with Emil Novák-Tót, an organisational design consultant with experience working with such data in the DEI space, to code and analyse the data according to the themes that emerged. It was clear from the data collected that all of them saw fear as a key barrier to making progress in DEI in organisations. The patterns that emerged showed us that there were a number of fears that people experienced when it came to DEI initiatives. These initial secondary themes were then grouped together into primary themes. Table 3.2 shows the primary and related secondary fears that emerged from the data. To test if these fears reflect sentiments more broadly,

Table 3.2 Primary and secondary fears of DEI initiatives

Primary fear	Related secondary fear
Fear of change	Fear of giving up one's position, power and space Fear of the unknown Fear of needing to do things differently Fear of the negative impact of DEI on the business Fear of losing one's freedom of thought/speech
Fear of getting it wrong	Fear of saying/doing the wrong thing Fear of being perceived as incompetent in matters of DEI Fear of having a negative or unintended impact Fear of not knowing enough about the DEI topic Fear of impact of failures or missteps on your (public) image Fear of not knowing the words and phrases

➤

Table 3.2 continued

Primary fear	Related secondary fear
Fear of discomfort	Fear of needing to discuss difficult topics about DEI with others Fear of losing one's self-image of being a good person Fear of the discomfort of addressing one's own bias
Fear of taking DEI-related actions	Fear of losing friendships and relationships Fear of being in situations of conflict or confrontation with colleagues when one addresses inequity, bias and discrimination that are witnessed or experienced Fear of addressing the inequity, bias and discrimination that are witnessed or experienced Fear of push-back or lack of commitment from decision makers
Fear of the personal consequences of taking DEI-related actions	Fear of being cancelled Fear of the impact of addressing bias on one's career Fear of DEI fatigue or burnout Fear of being perceived as the token hire Fear of the impact of addressing bias on how one is perceived by others Fear of the impact of being seen as the 'DEI/woke police' Fear for one's personal safety Fear of losing one's livelihood
Fear of the lack of positive impact of DEI efforts	Fear of the negative impact of performative DEI work Fear of not having a significant enough impact

I have conducted multiple workshops with leaders, employees and executive students from a range of different global organisations to understand if there was anything missing. Through these workshops, it was evident that the fears in Table 3.2 are reflective of the fears of DEI by people working in organisations.

In exploring their own fears of working with DEI, the interviewees also shared their own fears. It is worth noting that, after analysing the data, none of them raised a fear of discomfort when engaging in DEI efforts and only one person raised the fear of change and giving up their position, power and space that they occupy. Given the lack of adequate evidence, this latter aspect of fear was not included in the list. The lack of evidence in these two aspects tells us that those who are and have been working with DEI issues and initiatives are more comfortable with the topics themselves, and embrace the change needed to make our workplaces more diverse, equitable and inclusive. This is not to say that these fears don't arise among DEI professionals, but that these fears were not the primary ones raised by the interviewees. Table 3.3 shows the primary and secondary fears that DEI professionals experienced themselves.

Table 3.3 Primary and secondary fears of DEI initiatives experienced by DEI professionals

Primary fear	Secondary fear
Fear of getting it wrong	Fear of not knowing enough about the DEI topic Fear of saying/doing the wrong thing
Fear of taking DEI-related actions	Fear of push-back or lack of commitment from decision makers
Fear of the personal consequences of taking DEI-related actions	Fear of being cancelled Fear of the impact of addressing bias on one's career Fear of the impact of being seen as the 'DEI/woke police' Fear of losing one's livelihood Fear of DEI fatigue or burnout Fear of the impact of addressing bias on how one is perceived by others Fear for one's safety
Fear of the lack of positive impact of DEI efforts	Fear of not having a significant enough impact Fear of the negative impact of performative DEI work Fear of having a negative or unintended impact

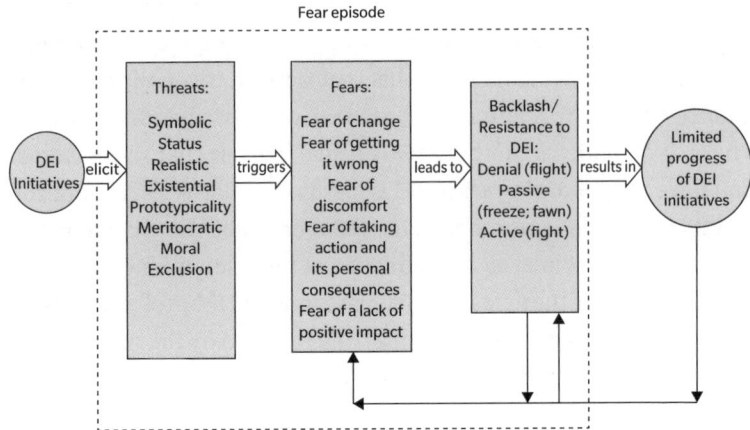

Figure 3.6 DEI fear episode

From the evidence presented, in the DEI space, there is plenty of fear. Fear is experienced by the well-represented and the underrepresented; by the privileged and the unprivileged; by those who are part of dominant groups and those who are part of marginalised groups; by those who advocate for DEI and those who don't. There is the fear of being discriminated against, of getting things wrong, of saying the wrong things or of feeling uncomfortable. There is the fear of being misunderstood or misrepresented, of being the lone voice, of being the token hire or even the fear of not doing anything. These fears prevent us from acting and keep us as bystanders, limiting progress towards nurturing inclusive workplaces. So, how can we let go of our fears and hold ourselves accountable to being inclusive at work?

Before we move forward to answer that question, it may be helpful to visualise what we have established until now through Figure 3.6.

Where do we go from here?

Having firmly established that fear – in its various forms – is the root cause of the backlash and resistance to DEI initiatives that we experience in and around us, the next step is learning how to let go of those fears. The fears of DEI that we have looked at until now do not serve us or our organisations and societies well, and hinder us from making progress. Letting go of our fears so that we don't react to the perceived threat of DEI with denial, passive or active backlash/ resistance is key to making progress. The good news is that research on neuroplasticity shows that we can transform how our brain perceives a threat and how we react to it. This transformation happens when we let go of our fears at the individual level, which is shown to lead to personal growth and development.[152] This in turn leads to greater empowerment, engagement and continuous improvement in organisations, and continuous renewal and equality in communities and societies.[153] What this means is that there is a positive ripple effect of letting go of our fears of DEI.

So, how do we let go of our fears of DEI? There are two main ways in which we can respond to fear: we can rely on interventions to manage the fear, or we can find ways to let go of the fear. The interventions to manage fear are many and well-known. They include everything from breathwork, to talking to others, to a walk in nature. These interventions help alleviate some of the physical stress reactions that occur in response to fear, such as increased blood pressure and heart rate, faster breathing, sweating, trembling and even digestive issues. While these provide some relief, they don't go far enough to address the root cause – the perception that DEI initiatives are a threat. To let go of the fears, we need to do more than just manage it. We need to take actions that move us away from seeing DEI initiatives as a threat so that we can let go of our fear of it. However, it seems like we are unsure about what to do to make this happen. In a survey of 852 professionals in the USA, about 41% of those surveyed said mid-level managers were not equipped to tackle criticism against DEI efforts, and 54% said front-line managers were not prepared to address pushback.[154] So, it seems like we need some guidance on how to address the fear that is causing this pushback to make progress.

Drawing on behavioural nudge theory,[155] nudges are interventions that gently steer us towards a desired action, and are used instead of direct instruction, enforcement or punishment. Nudges minimise resistance and confrontation, and are shown to be more effective in moving people towards the desired behaviours that are 'helpful outcomes for those people and society generally'.[156] Based on my prior research in this field, and experience working with numerous employees and leaders across multiple organisations, I believe that what we need to let go of our fears of DEI are the following five nudges (see Figure 3.7):

- *Openness* to let go of the fear of change.
- *Curiosity* to let go of the fear of getting it wrong.
- *Vulnerability* to let go of the fear of discomfort.
- *Courage* to let go of the fear of taking action and its personal consequences.
- *Resilience* to let go of the fear of a lack of positive impact.

In the rest of the book, we will explore the five nudges and their related tools that are needed to address the root cause of the fear by reframing how we look at DEI initiatives, viewing DEI not as a threat

Figure 3.7 Five nudges to let go of fear

but as an opportunity for the growth and development of ourselves, others and our organisations. By reframing how we look at DEI initiatives through these five nudges, we shift away from seeing DEI initiatives as a threat and, in turn, alleviate the most prevalent fears that this research has shown. This process begins with the need for us to be open and curious. With that, we can then be more vulnerable in engaging with the discomfort that can come with DEI topics. With this foundation, we are then able to be courageous to make change happen while being resilient to persevere in our efforts.

The nudges laid out in this book are aimed at empowering us, as individuals, to take action to make the cultural transformation happen. Cultural transformation does not happen through a strategy or roadmap, it happens through cultural change agents – you and me. As we have seen, everyone – even seasoned DEI professionals – experience fear of DEI. So, this book is for all of us who experience this fear. While change takes time, these nudges will give you what you need to address the backlash and resistance to DEI constructively to make change happen, both in yourself and in others. To make further progress with DEI requires us to let go of the elephant in the room – fear. This is where our journey begins.

Are you ready to learn how to let go of our fears of DEI initiatives and avoid feeling the dread of wondering if you 'can say that'?

Know your fears

The first step to letting go of our fear of DEI is to identify if fear in fact exists and what form the fear takes. So, let us begin with an honest reflection. Do you feel fearful of engaging in DEI initiatives at work?

- ☐ No: I am not fearful of engaging in DEI initiatives.
- ☐ Yes, but slightly: I am slightly fearful of engaging in DEI initiatives and also excited about engaging in DEI initiatives.
- ☐ Yes: I am quite fearful of engaging in DEI initiatives. It makes me uncomfortable.

➤

☐ Maybe: I am not sure if I am fearful or not. I need more time to reflect on this.

If you ticked yes or maybe, take a look at the list below and tick the sources of fear for yourself. Have you experienced any of the fears below?

Fear of change:

☐ Fear of giving up position, power and space that one occupies.
☐ Fear of the unknown.
☐ Fear of needing to do things differently.
☐ Fear of negative impact of DEI on the business.
☐ Fear of losing freedom of thought/speech.

Fear of getting it wrong:

☐ Fear of saying/doing the wrong thing.
☐ Fear of being perceived as incompetent in matters of DEI.
☐ Fear of having a negative or unintended impact.
☐ Fear of not knowing enough about the DEI topic.
☐ Fear of impact of failures or missteps on your (public) image.
☐ Fear of not knowing the words and phrases.

Fear of discomfort:

☐ Fear of needing to discuss difficult topics about DEI with others.
☐ Fear of losing one's self-image of being a good person.
☐ Fear of the discomfort of addressing one's own bias.

Fear of taking DEI-related actions:

☐ Fear of losing friendships and relationships.
☐ Fear of being in situations of conflict or confrontation with colleagues when one addresses inequity, bias and discrimination that are witnessed or experienced.
☐ Fear of addressing the inequity, bias and discrimination that are witnessed or experienced.
☐ Fear of pushback or lack of commitment from decision makers.

Fear of the personal consequences of taking DEI-related actions:

☐ Fear of being cancelled.
☐ Fear of the impact of addressing bias on one's career.
☐ Fear of DEI fatigue or burnout.
☐ Fear of being perceived as the token hire.
☐ Fear of the impact of addressing bias on how one is perceived by others.
☐ Fear of the impact of being seen as the 'DEI/woke police'.
☐ Fear for one's personal safety.
☐ Fear of losing one's livelihood.

Fear of the lack of positive impact of DEI efforts:

☐ Fear of the negative impact of performative DEI work.
☐ Fear of not having a significant enough impact.
☐ Fear of having a negative or unintended impact.

Are there any other fears of DEI that you have experienced that are not covered above? Make a note of them.

- -

Chapter 4

Let go of the fear of change with openness

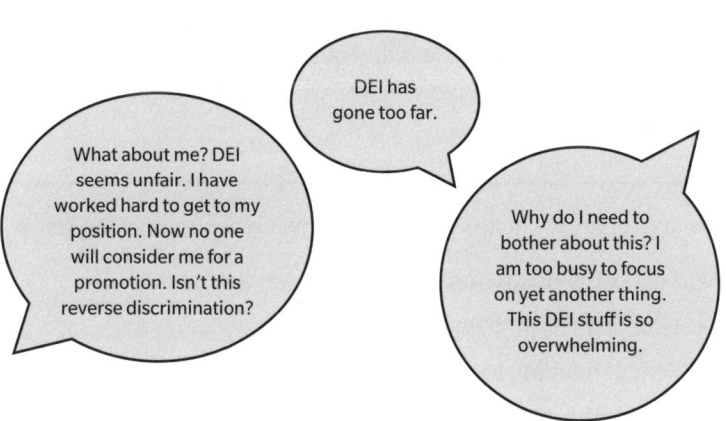

DEI has gone too far.

What about me? DEI seems unfair. I have worked hard to get to my position. Now no one will consider me for a promotion. Isn't this reverse discrimination?

Why do I need to bother about this? I am too busy to focus on yet another thing. This DEI stuff is so overwhelming.

The fear of change

'Change alone is unchanging.'

Heraclitus, Greek philosopher

We are creatures of habit and comfort. Even though we know that change will happen whether we want it or not, resisting change seems to be our default reaction. To many of us, DEI is new and feels like an unknown and so it is not surprising that, in the context of DEI, the fear of change shows up in many ways. We may be worried and anxious about the impact DEI initiatives will have on us, our position and the future opportunities available to us. We may even feel threatened by the need to give up space and power that we have enjoyed and held, or the right to express ourselves as we please. We may be fearful of what might be required from us. We may be worried that DEI may mean that we have to change the way that we have done things in the past. There is also the worry and anxiousness that DEI may have a negative impact on our businesses. This may prevent us from allocating resources towards DEI efforts if we are in decision-making roles. We may be worried that we are compromising on quality by hiring people who are different from who we have hired before, which may, in turn, jeopardise the success and sustainability of the business. All these fears are rooted in viewing the changes that come with DEI initiatives as a threat.

Fear of change encapsulates the following accompanying fears:

- Fear of giving up one's position, power and space.
- Fear of the unknown.
- Fear of needing to do things differently.
- Fear of the negative impact of DEI on the business.
- Fear of losing one's freedom of thought/speech.

Do you recognise any of these fears in yourself?

Once we have become aware of this fear, the question is – how do we let go of it? The answer involves addressing the root causes of the fear of change – the perceived loss, and the uncertainty and unknowns that come with DEI initiatives. To effectively address the root causes requires openness – openness to new and different experiences, ideas and ways of thinking and doing and, importantly, an openness to people who are different from us. This openness is key to moving us from feeling that DEI initiatives are a threat and instead to beginning to see them as an opportunity; an opportunity to see things differently, have richer interactions with others and to make decisions that are grounded in more robust viewpoints, perspectives and information. This, in turn, helps us to embrace change and to not be a naysayer.

So, how can we develop this openness?

Developing openness

Recognise your privilege

'I didn't choose to be white.'

'It's not my fault I was raised Christian.'

'Yes, I'm privileged, but I've still had to work really hard to get to where I am.'

To be open to DEI initiatives and lifting or creating space for people who are different from us, we first need to recognise our privilege. Why is recognising privilege necessary for openness? I believe that, once we become more aware of the lack of fairness in the systems and cultures around us and how that provides us with advantages that others do not have, it makes us more open to levelling the playing field. Privilege is a word that makes many of us feel uncomfortable. It may evoke feelings of guilt or shame, even anger and frustration. We may get defensive or feel as if we should feel bad about the unearned and earned advantages that we have over others.

Are you already wriggling in your seat, ready to close this book? Hold on for just a moment.

The negative narratives surrounding privilege may make us worry about what DEI initiatives mean for the positions, power and spaces that we have attained and enjoy because of unearned and earned advantages. You may have heard the activist adage by Malena Ernman, 'When you're used to privilege, equality feels like oppression.'

But what is privilege? Privilege is a system of 'automatic advantages and unearned assets available only to dominant groups of people'.[157] Our privilege refers to the aspects of our identity that we don't need to think about, the ones that others may need to consider. Privilege is assuming that just because something is not a problem for you, then it is not a problem for someone. If you have never considered how your skin colour or sexual orientation influence your life experiences – you have privilege in those areas. If we are privileged, we don't think about those aspects of our identity that give us advantages, opportunities or that shape the way we view the world and how others treat us. We may have always felt like we belong, and we assume that our life experiences are 'just how things are' and take them for granted. We may also assume that everyone has the same experiences as we do. Our privilege could also mean that we feel or assume that the reason why others don't get the same opportunities is because they are not good enough or don't work hard enough or even have made poor choices. Privilege is often invisible to those who have it.

When it comes to privilege, there are two things to keep in mind:

1 For unearned advantages, such as skin colour or biological sex, we continue to benefit from systems and cultures around us that favour people who share the same advantages.

2 For earned advantages, such as our education or job, acknowledging privilege does not mean negating the achievement or what it took to get there. Instead, recognising privilege means being open to reflect on how much harder it would have been for others who may have had to not only work hard but also overcome the lack of privilege.

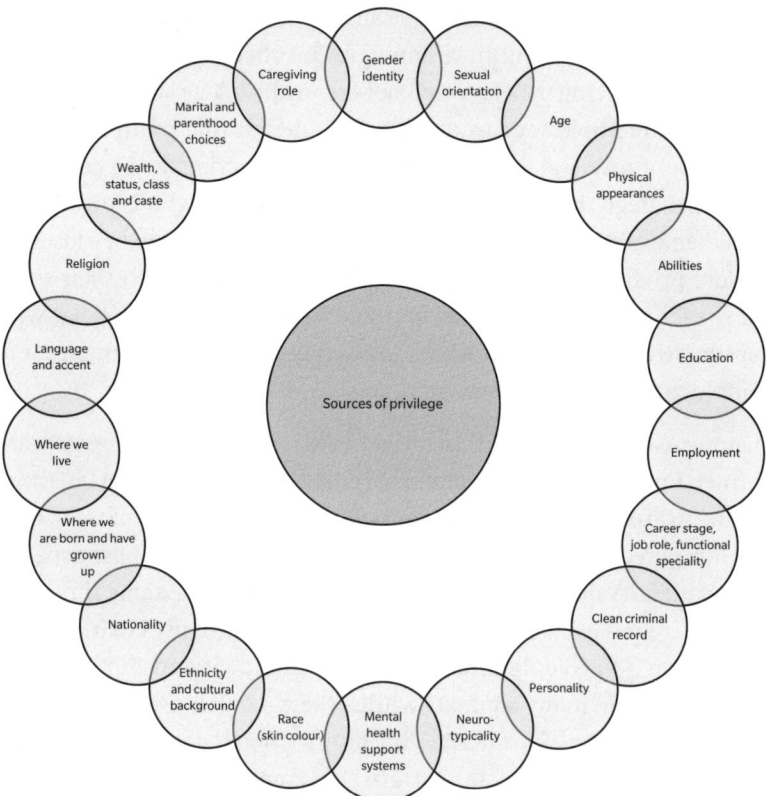

Figure 4.1 Sources of privilege

Privilege can come from many different sources, as we can see in Figure 4.1.

Privilege is fluid and relative, and not a monolith. We can gain or lose privilege over time. For example, through education, someone can gain privilege. Alternatively, if someone has an accident and becomes disabled, they can lose the privilege that came from being able-bodied. Privilege is also contextual. In some contexts, some aspects of our identity may accord us privilege while, in other contexts, those very same aspects of our identity may not. For example, our nationality may mean that, in some contexts, such as when we are in our home country, we have advantages like being able to vote or own land while, in other contexts, the very same nationality may mean that we receive additional scrutiny at immigration checkpoints. We can also experience having privilege and not having privilege simultaneously, and from multiple sources at once. This means that our privilege or the lack of privilege is compounded or intersectional. We can even have privilege through our proximity to someone who is privileged or when we modify the way we speak, dress or behave to be closer to where privilege lies. *Code-switching* is when people adjust their style of speech, appearance, behaviour and expressions in ways that will optimise the comfort of others in exchange for fair treatment and employment opportunities.

Let me use myself as an illustration. I am a 45-year-old Singaporean brown English-speaking woman of Indian ethnicity. I have a PhD and a 'Dr' in front of my name alongside being associate professor at a well-reputed university, Copenhagen Business School. These aspects of my identity don't exist in isolation, they exist at the same time and intersect with each other. Some of these aspects of my identity – my education, job role, language and accent and citizenship – accord me privilege in many contexts while others – my skin colour, gender identity and ethnicity – don't. This intersectional nature of privilege makes it difficult to say for certain that someone is only privileged and does not face disadvantages because of their identity. Privilege isn't static and it can certainly change over time. A few years after having completed my PhD, there was an opportunity to teach a Master's course. I approached the programme director and suggested that I would like to be considered for the role. He looked at me and said: 'Not until you have a lot more white hair.' I had solid teaching and peer evaluations but there I was – a woman of colour – being discriminated against on the basis of being 'too young'. While, at that time, my age acted against me, today, my age accords me many advantages of being 'more experienced'. I use these examples to emphasise that privilege is complex and isn't as simple as labelling people as 'privileged' or 'under-privileged/disadvantaged'. We need to better understand the nuances of privilege.

To understand privilege fully, we need to understand its intimate relationship with power. Privilege is 'unearned power, benefits, advantages, access and/or opportunities that exist for members of the dominant group(s) in society'.[158] Privilege gives a person or group power over others, and determines who has access to information/ knowledge, connections, experience and expertise, resources and decision making.

Power can be defined in many ways. One of those definitions is that power is the 'possession of control, authority or influence over others'.[159] Power is the ability to influence and make decisions that have an impact on others. History – and particularly colonisation and slavery – has had a profound influence on who holds privilege and power in our societies and organisations, and who does not. While you might be quick to say that colonisation and slavery are 'things of the past', its impact is still very much felt today in the power structures and culture that continue to define which groups hold privilege and power over others – based on race, class and gender.

In fact, in today's world, we see the prevalence of what is known as 'neo-colonialism' or the exerting of social, economic and political power on other communities, businesses and nations. In reality, we are far from being free from the clutches of colonialism. We see the continuation and reimposition of exploitation of indigenous communities in the mining and oil exploration industries across the African subcontinent, the Chinese Belt and Road initiative, and the French military and economic presence in its former colonies. These neo-colonial power structures create and uphold inequity and the systems of oppression (such as capitalism, patriarchy, white privilege and supremacy) that exist today. Those who are in positions of power continue to benefit from systems of oppression, and therefore find ways to continue to maintain these power systems. They resist any form of change that seeks to dismantle these systems that work in their favour. The many instances of resistance to DEI we have seen earlier in the book are evidence of this.

You may be thinking – how does this apply to me and my organisation? To understand how these power structures and dynamics influence your organisation, reflect on the following questions:

- Who holds decision-making power in your organisation? Can you describe them?
- Would you say that the employees who hold this power are disproportionately represented in positions of power or leadership?
- What aspects of your organisation's and society's culture reinforce or challenge power dynamics? Think about the hierarchy at play, how people communicate with each other and the assumptions, norms or expectations of what is considered to be appropriate behaviour. Is there a particular unsaid way in which things are done, the 'XYZ way'?

This imbalance in power is a barrier to achieving equity and fairness. So, how do we disrupt these imbalanced power structures, and decolonise our organisations? In her book, *How to End Injustice Everywhere*, Melanie Joy recommends the move from a 'power over' model to a 'power with' model in our interactions with other people. In the 'power over' model, 'we use power to exert dominance and control over others' whereas in the 'power with' model, 'power is used in the service of the whole – for the greater good of the relationship or group'.[160] Say that someone seeking a promotion intentionally undermines the efforts of a colleague in front of their manager. This is a good example of 'power over', also known as competitive power. The model operates from an 'either-or' mindset, meaning that either you gain/win or lose something – in the case of the example above, the promotion. In such a mindset, the possibility of both parties winning does not exist. On the other hand, an example of 'power with' would be when two colleagues work collaboratively, knowing that doing so will have a positive impact for their company as a whole. The 'power with' model operates from a 'both-and' mindset and is based on the belief that all individuals are equally worthy and deserve the same opportunities and treatment. In this mindset, all parties – the individuals and the organisation – make gains. To move to the 'power with' model, we need to:

- consider the impact of our choices on others and take that into account in our actions,
- help and enable others to be empowered through win–win collaborations,
- focus on integrity and dignity and move away from shame and contempt.

Once we have recognised our privilege, we need to ask ourselves how we are using our privilege to challenge the power structures at play. If you are in positions of privilege and power, what can you do to lift others and enable win–win collaborations? How can you use your privilege to drive change in your workplace? Who are you opening doors to? Whose voices are you inviting into conversations and considering as you make decisions? Who are you sponsoring and mentoring? What can you do to level the playing field and take actions to ensure that everyone has a fair chance?

Recognising our privilege is not easy but is imperative to letting go of fear. Are you open to recognising where your privilege lies?

Where does my privilege lie?

Below are a set of statements. If the statement applies to you, tick the box next to it.

Gender

- ☐ The leaders in my company are mostly people of my gender. The higher up in the corporate hierarchy, the more this is true.
- ☐ My leadership skills or work abilities are not questioned by others based on my gender.
- ☐ My manager is a person of my gender.
- ☐ When completing surveys/forms for work, my gender is an option on the drop-down menu.

➤

- [ ] It is rare that I am interrupted during meetings.
- [ ] It is extremely rare that someone explains things to me in a way that makes me feel less competent.
- [ ] It is rare that someone takes my ideas during a meeting, reshares them and gains greater acceptance of the idea than when I shared my ideas.
- [ ] I am not told that I am in the 'wrong' toilet.

Sexual orientation

- [ ] I do not worry that if people know my sexual orientation and/or gender identity there will be emotional, physical or psychological consequences.
- [ ] I do not need to hide who I love out of fear of judgement or, worse, criminal persecution.
- [ ] I can bring my partner to a company event without concern of being judged or treated differently.
- [ ] No one believes my sexual orientation and/or gender identity was 'caused' by sin, disease or abuse.
- [ ] No one believes that my sexual orientation can be 'reversed' through therapy, medication or meeting the right person.

Age

- [ ] I have never been refused an opportunity or job because of my age.
- [ ] It is rare that people dismiss my view citing that I am 'too young' or 'lacking life experience' because of my age.
- [ ] I have never been refused a job because 'there were many other applicants with much more experience'.
- [ ] I have never been made fun of or mocked for not knowing something current.
- [ ] Others don't assume I don't know things simply because of my age.

Abilities and neurotypicality

- [ ] I can easily get into any building or room that I need to enter.
- [ ] I have never been stared at, or been left out, due to a disability.

☐ People do not treat me as if I am less capable of doing my work because of the look or ability of my body.

☐ Strangers do not ask me what happened to my body.

☐ Workplaces and work tools do not have to be modified to meet my needs.

☐ I have never had to hide my invisible disabilities when applying for a job.

☐ The ways in which I think and learn are considered 'normal'.

☐ I am comfortable looking at others in their eyes.

☐ Open offices do not bother me.

Appearances

☐ I do not have to alter my natural hair to be seen to be professional.

☐ I do not have to carefully choose what I wear to ensure that I am taken seriously.

☐ The leaders in my company and I are about the same height.

☐ I have never felt judged because of my weight.

☐ I have never felt that I have not got a job or promotion because of my weight.

Education, employment, criminal record and personality

☐ My educational background is viewed as prestigious.

☐ I am rarely asked questions about why I made the educational choices I did.

☐ I have a stable job with a salary that helps me live comfortably and provide for my family.

☐ I do not have a criminal record.

☐ I have never been told that my personality is unsuitable for a job.

☐ I have never been told that my personality is eccentric.

Race, ethnicity, culture, nationality, language/accent and religion

☐ I grew up in the country I currently live in.

☐ I am never stopped at immigration queues when travelling for work because of my nationality.

☐ I have never had to justify my entry into a country.   ➤

☐ I have never felt judged or had people give me suspicious looks because of my skin colour.

☐ I have never had to explain and defend where I am from and/or answer the follow-up question: 'Where are you *actually* from?'

☐ I can usually find people of my ethnic background in top management and leadership roles in my organisation.

☐ The official language of my company is one that I am fluent in.

☐ My accent is well understood by my colleagues, and I am rarely asked to repeat myself because of it.

☐ I have never felt like hiding or changing my name.

☐ I can go shopping alone most of the time, being sure that I will not be followed or closely watched by store employees because of my ethnic background.

☐ I can take a job with an employer who believes in equal opportunity employment without others thinking that I got my job only because of my ethnic background.

☐ I have never felt like the 'token' hire.

☐ I have never been the first person of my ethnicity to be hired to my team or organisation.

☐ I have never felt like I need to work much harder than others.

☐ I have never been asked to speak on behalf of a whole group of people from the same race, ethnic or religious background that I am from.

☐ I can be fairly sure that I will not have to work on the religious holidays that are important to me.

☐ Most of my managers and colleagues are familiar with my faith.

☐ Food that does not violate my religious or environmental beliefs can be easily found in the office canteen and at work-related events.

☐ I do not need to explain my food choices to others.

☐ Most people do not consider my religious practices to be 'weird' or 'old-fashioned'.

☐ I do not need to worry about how I would be judged by wearing clothing or symbols of my religion to work.

Marital and parenthood choices

- ☐ My marital choices are rarely met with disapproval.
- ☐ I can marry my partner legally.
- ☐ Who I am married to makes it easier for me to get access to spaces and people.
- ☐ I receive benefits from my workplace for my spouse and myself.
- ☐ I am rarely asked when I will have a baby.
- ☐ I did not have to juggle work and childcare responsibilities for my children. Someone else is the primary caregiver for my children.
- ☐ I outsource childcare responsibilities to my partner or spouse.
- ☐ I have access to good quality and affordable childcare.
- ☐ I work for a company with parenthood policies that I can avail.
- ☐ I am not penalised for using my company's parenthood policies.
- ☐ If I have children and a successful career, I am rarely asked how I manage to balance my professional and private lives.

Wealth, status, class and caste

- ☐ I do not have to worry about my basic needs of food and shelter.
- ☐ I have never been homeless.
- ☐ I have never had to skip a meal to save money.
- ☐ My parents went to college/university.
- ☐ My parents have been able to help me with writing job/college applications.
- ☐ The majority of the kids in the area(s) where I grew up went to college/university.
- ☐ I have easy access to technology and the internet.
- ☐ I have enough space to work at home.
- ☐ I have a family to whom I go home every evening.
- ☐ I have a good social network of friends.
- ☐ I have health insurance and access to good quality healthcare.
- ☐ I have easy access to mental health care, should I need it.
- ☐ I live in a country with a strong and stable political system.

- -

Having completed the above exercise, reflect on your privilege. Think about the following questions and pen down your reflections in your notebook.

- Do you have privilege?
- In which categories do your privileges lie? Reflect on how they give you an advantage over others.
- Which sources of your privilege are unearned, and which aspects are earned?
- Which sources of your privilege are fluid and dependent on the context and situation in which you are?
- In which situations and contexts do you feel that you do not have as much privilege as others? How does that impact you?

Debunk the myths

'There's a lot of immigration happening which means there's a lot of unknowns coming into these countries – unknown cultures, unknown ideas, unknown beliefs, unknown food, unknown ways of being and knowing. And the idea that those unknowns can start to not just be included, but start to centre themselves in the decision-making process and how our systems are run is a really scary prospect. Because then you're going from something that is familiar, albeit messed up and that doesn't necessarily work the best, to something that potentially you're not going to benefit from. And it's no longer going to feel like your country.'

DEI expert

In our organisations, we often hold certain beliefs that are nothing but myths waiting to be debunked. While there are many such myths about DEI, let us take a look at three of the most prevalent and how we can debunk these myths to be more open to DEI initiatives.

Myth 1: Our organisation is meritocratic. We only hire the very best people for the job. Hiring people from underrepresented backgrounds means compromising competencies and quality. Women and other 'minorities' just need to work harder to get ahead.

Have you heard these comments, or perhaps even thought of them yourself?

'Diversity, Equity and Inclusion has gone too far. People who work hard get ahead, simple. If someone isn't getting ahead, they just aren't competent.'

'I do not see colour or gender; I just hire the best person.'

As we have seen, meritocracy, the belief that success is solely based on merit and hard work, is a myth. We would like to think that our workplaces are meritocratic and that the people who are hired for roles, including ourselves, are chosen purely on the basis of merit. While there is no doubt that merit plays a part in people's career progress, we cannot ignore the role that privilege and bias play. Privilege and bias cause decision makers, systems and our organisational culture to favour some people over others. Our privileges and the bias around us means that it is likely that we have had advantages over others that have made it 'easier' for us – relative to others – to get an education, have access to a network, get a job and move up the corporate ladder. This means that people who have the same or similar competencies but don't have the same advantages often don't get a fair chance to be considered for a job or promotion.

Think about an Ivy League or similar education. Such an education is available to only a few: those who have the financial means available, those fortunate or talented enough to obtain a scholarship, legacy admissions or those who are eligible for bursary funding. An Ivy League education offers a host of advantages – from job opportunities to a network with the 'elite' that one can leverage throughout one's career, and don't forget the higher starting salaries that come with Ivy League degrees.

Going further, this bias also means that we hold some people to different standards compared to others. This means that women and people of colour have to work harder to prove that they are competent, what is known as the 'prove-it-again-bias'.[161] Did you know that 40% of black women say they need to provide more evidence of their competence, compared to 28% of white women and 14% of men.[162] In the book, *Leading Through Bias*, the authors write, 'When we believe that the world is just, we also tend to believe that inequalities reflect a meritocratic process. This means that we assume that the poorer outcomes for underrepresented groups are due to their inadequate competencies; that inequity and inequality are the result of lack of skills, and not a result of our biased decision making. This allows us to maintain our belief that we live in a fair world rather than having to actually address the inequities that exist.'[163]

Myth 2: DEI does not concern or benefit me.

There is plenty of evidence that shows that everyone stands to benefit from an inclusive and equitable workplace where everyone can be themselves and feel like they belong. In such an organisation, we see improved employee well-being, higher employee satisfaction, lower turnover rates, increased productivity, higher employee engagement, better decision making, enhanced innovation, higher employee satisfaction, lower turnover rates, increased productivity, higher employee engagement and, in turn, improved organisational performance. Despite this supporting research and data, it may be hard to believe that DEI benefits everyone, especially if we are part of the dominant group whose historic privileges and advantages suddenly seem like they are under threat. To show that even for those who are part of the dominant group, DEI has benefits, let's look at the concept of toxic masculinity that plagues our workplaces and society.

Toxic masculinity is 'a cultural concept of manliness that glorifies stoicism, strength, virility, and dominance, and that is socially maladaptive or harmful to mental health'.[164] The culture of toxic masculinity results in extreme and overt misogyny, homophobia and patriarchal systems, as well as behaviours that include the need to dominate, not showing weakness, sexual entitlement and aggression and controlling behaviour. The culture of toxic masculinity can present as bullying or aggression towards others to maintain power or refusal to admit mistakes to avoid appearing weak. More so, it influences our ideas of leaders and leadership qualities, who should be 'listened to' and who has power and authority.

It is easy to see how this culture of toxic masculinity negatively impacts women by centring power and control with men, but it is important to note that it is also damaging for men. From a young age, men often feel immense pressure to conform to the stereotypical profile of what it means to be a man. They may not feel comfortable showing emotions outside of pride and anger, considered to be appropriate masculine emotions. In the workplace, they might be less empathetic to colleagues. Fathers who want to participate more fully in child or home-care responsibilities are sometimes met with disapproval and judgement. Some are even questioned about why their partner (usually assumed to be a woman) isn't available to do this. The comments can sound like these:[165]

'Can't your wife do that?'

'I always put my career first, and my family turned out fine.'

'Must be nice to go home early.' (Said to a father after he said he was leaving to take care of his sick child.)

DEI initiatives that focus on anti-harassment, parental leave and flexible work options along with nurturing an inclusive culture aim to ensure that everyone can show up with our intersectional identities – including those outside of the rigid confines of a culture of toxic masculinity – and be valued, heard and respected without discrimination, and feel like we belong.

Myth 3: There is nothing wrong with our organisation. People just need to fit in with our culture.

Most of us associate being biased with being 'a bad person'. The truth is, anyone who has a brain is biased. Our brain receives an immense amount of information every second. To consciously process this information would be so overwhelming that we rely on heuristics, algorithms and mental shortcuts. These mental shortcuts form our biases. Biases exist in us, in others and by default, in our culture, structures, systems, policies and practices. After all, our organisational culture, structures, systems, policies and practices are developed and created by our biased brains.

Biases take many forms. We can hold biases that are based on aspects of a person's identity such as gender, race or age, or based on how we process information in various situations. Those biases include affinity bias, intuition bias, confirmation bias, groupthink and others. The range and number of biases that exist in human beings is large. You may find it interesting to note that, according to the 2023 UN Gender Social Norms Index (GSNI) report, close to 9 out of 10 men *and* women worldwide hold fundamental biases against women, and 2 out of 5 people believe that men make better business executives than women do.[166]

Bias also leads organisations to 'hire for fit', a practice I refer to as the 'cookie cutter phenomenon' in my book, *The Art of Active Allyship*. Organisations have moulds or prototypes – cookie cutters – that are used as a basis for what an ideal leader, executive or employee looks like. Bias leads us to continue hiring people who fit within that cookie cutter form, hiding behind the excuse of 'hiring for fit', which preserves comfort, familiarity and homogeneity. We assume that people who fit the cookie cutter are capable while others are a 'risky hire'. This results in us underestimating what others are capable of and the value they can add. We should be looking for ways to 'hire to add' rather than 'fit'. Hiring and promoting people from different backgrounds, experiences and perspectives – whose values align with the organisation's values – adds significant value to the organisation and the people in them.

If these myths are holding us back, how do we debunk them?

Start by asking yourself if you hold stereotypes or assumptions about a particular social group. If you are a manager, do you acknowledge and leverage differences in your team? Then, use your answers to help you become more aware of your unconscious assumptions – your bias.

The fact that everyone is biased is not an excuse to continue doing things the same way they have been done before or to hold on to the beliefs we have held in the past. We need to question our own beliefs. We need to be critical of what we view as 'normal' or 'just how things are'. For this, we need to be willing to challenge our beliefs.

If you are ready, start by increasing awareness of your biases. You can do this through a range of practical actions. One way is by gaining a deeper understanding into the different forms of bias. There are plenty of resources out there to help you learn about the various biases – books, podcasts and articles. Once you become aware of biases that you hold, you may notice them more frequently. Don't worry, this does not mean you've suddenly become more biased, only more aware of biases that have always been there. The next step is to take actions to challenge the biases.

Are you ready to debunk the myths? Here are a few actions you can take.

Rely on bias buddies

Bias buddies are people with whom you are comfortable having con-versations about biases you have noticed in yourself. Bias buddies can provide a safe space to have conversations without feeling judged or threatened. They should challenge your biases as well as question your beliefs and ask why you see things in a particular way. Engaging in these rich conversations helps us to critically review our beliefs.

Avoid 'othering' others

Othering is a phenomenon in which some individuals or groups are defined and labelled as not fitting in with the norms of a social group. Othering is a 'set of dynamics, processes, and structures that engender marginality and persistent inequality across any of the full range of human differences based on group identities.'[167] This creates an 'us vs them' mentality that influences how people perceive and treat those who are viewed as being part of the in-group versus those who are seen as being part of the out-group. We can other people on the basis of gender, sexual orientation, race, ethnicity, socioeconomic status, disability and religion, among others.

How do you know if you are othering someone or a group of people?

- You attribute positive qualities to people who are like you and negative qualities to people who are different from you.
- You believe that people who are different from you or your social group pose a threat to you or your way of life.
- You are distrustful of people in a social group even though you don't know anyone from that group.
- You refuse to interact with people because they are different from you or your social group.
- You believe that people outside your social group are not as intelligent, skilled or as special as you and your group.
- You associate some people only with their relationship with specific social groups without giving any thought to them as individuals.

To avoid othering, become aware of the stereotypes or 'cookie cutters' that you may use in your interactions with others and challenge them. This could be when you are interacting with colleagues or meeting a candidate for a role in your team. In the decisions you make on who you hire, promote or give opportunities to, ask yourself critical questions about how and why you arrived at a decision, and what biases could have been at play. When we other people, we are prioritising our individual needs and our comfort, rather than looking at what is good for the team or organisation. When we engage in othering, we engage in behaviours and attitudes that reflect our comfort with people who are like us in terms of our gender identity, age, race, etc. At the same time, we also engage in behaviours and attitudes that reflect our discomfort with people who are different from us. We need to move away from a focus on just ourselves, 'I' and 'my', to focus on what is good for the community as a whole, 'us' and 'we'.

Actively seek out alternative perspectives

The proverb 'birds of a feather flock together' has some truth to it – human beings love being with people who think like they do, which is known as homophily. When researchers asked groups of executives if their organisations have become more or less diverse in thought, the responses showed that nearly everyone has witnessed an increase in divergent attitudes, perspectives and values in the workplace. Yet, when they asked the same people if their own professional networks have become more diverse, their responses were a mix of 'No' and 'I don't know.'[168] Even though our workplaces are becoming increasingly diverse, our nature is to stick to people who think like us. This leads to homogeneous echo chambers that limit our access and exposure to the alternative perspectives that enrich the way we look at the world. In the words of Albert Einstein, 'We cannot solve our problems with the same thinking we used when we created them.'

Challenge yourself to be open to different perspectives and views. Question norms. Norms are the often invisible and unsaid ways in which things are done and what is considered to be acceptable or preferred. Ask yourself why these norms exist, and if they favour some people and not others. Intentionally seek out alternative perspectives that challenge your worldview and provide a different take on the situation so that the decision you are making is based on wider and more robust information. This can mean having a conversation with someone with a different view or reading or listening to content where the viewpoint is different from your own. Your decision or view on an issue may or may not change as a result of these alternative perspectives. The objective is not to always change your opinion or decision but to know that our views and decisions are more thoroughly informed. One of my favourite phrases is 'tell me more'. This simple phrase helps me engage in rich discussions and conversations and to see things from a different perspective. Every time we engage in a way that challenges our pre-held beliefs, we are creating new mental models and 'overriding' the previous ones. This is an essential part of developing an inclusive mindset.

Tell me more. Try it.

Move from a scarcity mindset to an abundance mindset

'I think that any talk of reverse discrimination is about a fear of losing power and control. Even when it's said as a joke. A lot of times, it's meant as, "Oh, now it's going to be hard to be a white guy here. There's going to be lack of job opportunities for men" or saying, "Is it suddenly going to be a liability to be a man?" It comes out in a lot as jokes but sometimes it's clearly articulated as critique.'

HR leader

To develop this openness towards the diversity of people and DEI initiatives that aim to transform our culture, we have to move away from seeing our workplaces as finite, consisting of only jobs, roles and promotions. When we lack openness, it is easy to assume that the purpose of DEI initiatives is to only address diversity in representation. When we view DEI efforts as a zero-sum game, we are left with a *scarcity mindset*.

Stephen Covey coined the term scarcity mindset, and the opposite – abundance mindset – in his best-selling book, *The 7 Habits of Highly Effective People*. Scarcity mindset refers to when we see our workplaces as a finite pizza or a pie so that, if one person takes a piece, it leaves less for everyone else. Most of us have been conditioned to have this scarcity mindset in the DEI space as a result of 'quick fix' efforts like affirmative action and quotas. We have been conditioned to believe that there are limited resources and choices available to us in uncertain environments where decisions are made through social comparison on who is more worthy to receive access to those limited resources and choices.[169] In the context of DEI, this means that, with a focus on increasing the level of representation of underrepresented groups, and given that promotions and raises are scarce, we see such DEI initiatives as a threat to the resources and choices available to us. Scarcity mindset is what leads to the 'power over' models of competitiveness for positions and promotions. This is what we see play out in the backlash and resistance to DEI with DEI being referred to as 'reverse discrimination'. In contrast, an abundance mindset refers to the view that there are plenty of resources for everybody.

What is the consequence of a scarcity mindset? Well, one consequence is that we end up pulling others down as we try to rise up. Tall Poppy Syndrome refers to the act of attacking, resenting, disliking, criticising or cutting down others because of their achievements and/or success. The name is derived from the idea that the tallest poppy must be cut down to keep the field uniform. The Tallest Poppy 2023[170] was an international study across 103 countries that looked at thousands of working women from all demographics and professions to determine how their mental health, well-being, engagement and performance are affected by interactions with their clients, colleagues and leaders.

The study revealed that women – nearly 9 out of 10 of us – were being 'cut down' in the workplace, feeling the need to downplay their achievements, being left out/ignored, being undermined, having their achievements dismissed or having others take credit for their success. If you are wondering who is doing the cutting, the study finds that men in higher leadership positions are more likely to penalise or undermine women below them in the hierarchy due to their success. But it is not just men. Women are more likely to cut down peers. What is the consequence of this 'cutting down'? The study shows that it leads to stress, burnout, negative impact on mental health and lower self-confidence.

So, how do we move from a scarcity mindset to an abundance mindset?

Reflect honestly and deeply

To shift our mindset first requires us to get a deeper understanding about where our scarcity mindset comes from. The next time you have feelings of contempt and insecurity come up when faced with DEI initiatives such as the introduction of equitable hiring practices, Pride month celebrations or pay-equity exercises, ask yourself the following questions:

- What am I feeling?
- Why am I feeling this?
- Where is it coming from?
- Am I feeling jealous or insecure?
- Are my thoughts reflecting biases against a particular person or group?

Understand what DEI actually means

As we have seen earlier, 'reverse discrimination' is a commonly used phrase by those opposing DEI initiatives. But what is it referring to? Reverse discrimination is assumed to be a form of discrimination affecting members of a majority instead of a minority. While DEI efforts aim to address systemic discrimination, it is often misunderstood that DEI efforts that aim to remove systemic barriers and bias for underrepresented and underestimated groups on the basis of race or gender, for example, are forms of 'reverse discrimination'. Examples of this 'reverse discrimination' can include making decisions in favour of minority groups solely based on race, or recruiting or promoting women solely based on their sex or gender. It stems from the fear that efforts to address historical inequities may inadvertently lead to discrimination against majority groups. There is no such thing as 'reverse discrimination', even if DEI efforts feel like they are for those who are from privileged and well-represented groups. The use of the phrase 'reverse discrimination' arises from a misunderstanding of the goals of diversity and inclusion initiatives. DEI initiatives do not aim to discriminate against any group but to promote fairness and equity for all. In the process of levelling the playing field, it can feel like it is discriminating against those who have enjoyed advantages.

Imagine that you have two children and, for many years, you favoured one over the other. Every week, you buy 10 cookies and, for years, every week you gave those 10 cookies to your favoured child while your other child got none. Realising this is unfair, you decide that, from then on, you will divide the 10 cookies equally between the 2 children. To the child who was accustomed to receiving 10 cookies every week, this seems unfair. That child feels entitled to *all* the cookies though, in reality, the distribution was not fair to begin with. If we *really* wanted to be fair, we should give the second child a greater proportion of the cookies to make up for the historical imbalance. This analogy is inspired by a LinkedIn post by Dr Robert Livingston, Harvard social psychologist and author of *The Conversation: How Seeking and Speaking the Truth About Racism Can Radically Transform Individuals and Organizations*. When we have enjoyed privilege, it is easy to see DEI efforts as unfair because we stand to 'lose' what was never ours to hoard in the first place. DEI efforts are not about denying anyone cookies but rather about addressing systemic inequities to make who has privilege and power fairer – to make sure there are enough cookies for everyone.

We have developed a false understanding of inclusion while also underestimating the role of equity in achieving inclusion. This misunderstanding stems from the assumption that inclusion means that those who are privileged continue to enjoy their privilege while marginalised groups are invited in but expected to conform to the dominant norms and power structures. The end goal is for marginalised folks to become integrated into the world of the privileged, becoming like them. That is not inclusion, it is assimilation. Inclusion is about dismantling structures and cultures that have benefited some and not others. Inclusion is about ensuring equity and fairness; about levelling the playing field. So, yes, those of us who have enjoyed privilege need to open up the space that we occupy, add more seats to the table and even modify the table or design a new one to make it fairer for others. A few examples come to mind – disabled parking spots, Employee

Resource Groups (ERGs), gender-neutral toilets and LGBTQ+ friendly spaces. These examples, which are inclusionary to underrepresented and marginalised groups, might be considered exclusionary by dominant groups. In these instances, exclusion is about rebalancing power and opportunities; this is equity in action and necessary to achieve a more just and fairer world. These DEI efforts help people from these groups feel a sense of inclusion from belonging in a space where they can be themselves without fear of harassment. These efforts open up spaces to be inclusive to people from marginalised groups without really taking away much space from the privileged.

It is important to keep in mind that DEI initiatives, even when they seem to be for the benefit of a marginalised group, can benefit everyone. Quiet spaces benefit neurodivergent and introverted employees but also anyone who may need space to re-energise by stepping away from the hustle and bustle of open-office spaces. A prayer or faith room benefits anyone who would like to spend some time in meditation or reflection. Alcohol-free events or ensuring the availability of non-alcoholic drinks at events benefits pregnant women, someone who is a recovering alcoholic, someone who is driving home later that day and those who don't drink for health or religious reasons, but it also benefits women by reducing the risk of harassment that often takes place at events with alcohol. It means that no one has to explain why they don't drink, freeing them from the burden of sharing aspects of their identity that they might not feel comfortable sharing.

Another great example is the 'curb cut effect'.[171] In the 1940s, pavements in the USA were modified to create a sloped section by cutting into the curbs of the pavement to provide better accessibility for the disabled. What people discovered was that the curb cuts had benefits beyond the scope of what it was originally intended for, the disabled. It also benefited cyclists, parents or caregivers pushing buggies and people pushing luggage. This created 'unexpected but welcome positive externalities. In short, curb cuts created more inclusive environments that benefited everyone and became standard practice for U.S. civil engineering. DEI initiatives strive to do the same.'[172] Can you think of any other DEI initiatives that have benefited a wider community than initially intended?

Reflect on the opportunities for you, your team and your company

As we have seen, DEI initiatives benefit all. They have been shown to improve engagement, belonging and inclusion, health and well-being, performance and retention – all good outcomes for individuals, teams and organisations.

More diversity in teams, with people who bring a variety of perspectives and experiences, consider information more thoroughly and accurately,[173] results in faster problem solving,[174] as well as higher quality decisions and intellectual output.[175] A diverse team is not enough. It should be emphasised that it is also about ensuring that there is an inclusive culture that supports this variety of perspectives. It is the merger of these perspectives that results in synergistic benefits. In fact, employees' overall experiences of inclusion may help explain 49% of problem solving in teams and 18% of employee innovation.[176] Companies with such an inclusive culture and accompanying D&I policies are shown to have a 59.1% increase in creativity, innovation and openness.[177]

There is more. Just a 10% increase in perceptions of inclusion reduces absenteeism, adding nearly one day a year in work attendance per employee.[178] A 2016 report by the European Commission draws on studies that show that having LGBTQ+-supportive policies reduces incidences of discrimination, thereby improving psychological health and increasing job satisfaction, while also improving relationships between LGBTQ+ employees and their colleagues.[179] The US Department of Labor[180] found that employers who addressed the organisational inequity of people with a disability – through conscious efforts to hire talent with disabilities, engaging in awareness building programmes for all employees, offering mentor and mentee opportunities, implementing skill-building programmes and making space for diverse talent to hold roles at all levels – saw a 90% increase in employee retention.[181] While diverse organisations certainly attract more diverse talent, it is also worth noting that employees' experiences of inclusion play a key role in improved job satisfaction and commitment to their employer.[182] This is in addition to greater trust,[183] employee engagement and retention.[184]

There are significant benefits that come from DEI work. DEI enables you to be a better leader, more efficient and make better decisions. The next time you find yourself resisting DEI efforts, or worrying about the extra 'work', ask yourself this: what is the business case for exclusion?

Decentre yourself

'I think it is the fear of difference – fear of someone who looks different and who behaves differently. There might be something that we perhaps do not understand in that person. That fear of differences drives people's actions, and those actions can show up as just not being able to engage at all. Perhaps, it's just running away from that situation or that individual.'

DEI expert

'What about me? There are no opportunities left for white men like me.'

Whataboutery is the technique or practice of responding to an accusation or difficult question by making a counter-accusation or raising a different issue altogether. We see this happen often in DEI discussions. When topics about sexual harassment or assault against women are raised, 'whatabouters' counter with, 'What about men who get harassed and sexually assaulted?' or #NotAllMen. When the Black Lives Matter movement gained traction in 2020 following the murder of George Floyd in the USA, social media erupted with #AllLivesMatter. These whataboutery responses may come from feeling personally attacked or the fear that such conversations will lead to actions that address discrimination.

Whataboutery is a logical fallacy that prevents us from having rich discussions about a topic. It deflects focus and distracts the conversation, steering it towards another, maybe related, topic. This technique is often used to avoid having conversations about what a person may consider to be a 'sensitive' or polarising topic such as racism or sexism.

'I have never experienced this. Are you sure that is what happened? I find it hard to believe.'

The above is an example of gaslighting, a way to psychologically manipulate (a person) 'usually over an extended period of time that causes the victim to question the validity of their own thoughts, perception of reality, or memories and typically leads to confusion, loss of confidence and self-esteem, uncertainty of one's emotional or mental stability.'[185]

In a workplace context, gaslighting occurs when a colleague or manager manipulates a person to the point that they begin to question their own sanity, memory or perceptions. The gaslighter can do this by denying past events, downplaying the person's emotions or retelling events so that the blame falls away from them. According to Vicki Salemi, a career expert and coach for Monster.com: 'Gaslighting at work is when a person – typically a colleague or manager – invalidates what you know to be true, forcing you to question the facts and, ultimately, yourself and your ability to do your job. In other words, they're twisting (either accidentally or intentionally) information, words and behaviour to make you feel confused, trivialise feelings and block you from success.'[186]

Both whataboutery and gaslighting are examples of ways in which we centre ourselves.

How, then, can we decentre ourselves?

Let data and evidence drive your reactions

The next time someone raises an issue related to discrimination in the workplace, resist the temptation to counter it with a sentence starting with 'What about . . . ?'. Remember that this is not about you nor is it an attack on you. So, you don't have to respond to deny, dismiss or doubt their experience. Remember that no discrimination is acceptable, and just because it is not your experience, does not mean that it did not happen to someone else. This is the very definition of having privilege.

Instead, be open to learning if the discrimination is reflective of a wider problem that needs a systemic and cultural approach. You can do this by collecting data and evidence. Employee engagement surveys are a great way to identify if certain underrepresented groups experience lower levels of inclusion and belonging than others. Having conversations with employees across different intersectional identities is another way to collect qualitative data and get a good pulse of how people are feeling.

When in doubt, seek out the data. If you feel that your company is only hiring women or people from a particular ethnic group, seek out the data. I recall having a conversation with a male senior leader who had received a complaint from one of the leaders in his team that the company was hiring only women. So, he got the data and addressed it with his team. It turns out that there certainly was an increase in the number of women hired compared to before, but this was only 30% of the total hires; 70% of the new hires were still men. Because of something known as frequency illusion effect, things sometimes seem to be one way when, in reality, the numbers show otherwise.

Create inclusive spaces

When we have privilege, the spaces we are in cater to us. This can be everything from the national holidays from work that align with the festivals we celebrate, to physical spaces that are easy for us to move through and to toilets that align with our gender identity. People who are part of well-represented groups enjoy the privilege of the inclusive culture of the spaces we are in, while those who are from marginalised groups do not enjoy the same. In her book *Invisible Women: Exposing Data Bias in a World Designed for Men*, Caroline Criado Perez uses data to force us to consider a world created and built by men – from the crash test dummies to the temperature in our offices to the floor space allocated for female toilets in public areas.[187]

This leads to people from marginalised groups needing to 'fit' into structures and systems that were not built for them. This is what Kenji Yoshino calls 'covering'. In his book, *Covering*, he defines 'covering' as 'a strategy through which individuals with known outsider identities modulate or edit their identities to blend into the mainstream'.[188] It is closely related to the concept of code-switching that we saw earlier. Covering shows up in many ways. A father may have an ambiguous placeholder in his calendar for the times he coaches his child's football team to avoid mentioning it to colleagues for fear of being seen as less committed or working less than is expected. Racial minorities are pressured to 'act white' by changing their names, languages or cultural practices. Women are told to 'play like men' at work. Gays are asked not to engage in public displays of same-sex affection. The devout are instructed to minimise expressions of faith, and individuals with disabilities are urged to conceal the paraphernalia that permit them to function. This is also related to the concept of camouflaging, in which neurodivergent individuals adopt and change their behaviour to better navigate societal expectations like engaging in small talk, participating in chatty lunches and attending team events.

When the spaces we are in cater for us, we occupy a disproportionate amount of 'space'. That can be a disproportionate time speaking in meetings, taking up a position on a panel where we may not be the best person or the frequency with which we are selected for opportunities in the company. By taking up more space, it may mean that others who are equally qualified but have less privilege do not get a chance.

You can reduce the space you occupy through microaffirmations. These microaffirmations all indicate value, respect and build inclusion:

- Invite people whose voice and perspectives have not been heard. Ask yourself – whose perspective is missing in the room?
- Offer your seat on a panel or in a speaker series to a colleague.

- Demand from organisers of events that they should have a more diverse representation of speakers.
- Suggest names of competent and qualified colleagues and team members from marginalised and underrepresented groups for opportunities.

If the previous actions to reduce the space you occupy have made you wonder if doing this will reduce your visibility and relevance to the organisation, take a few minutes to visualise the negative outcomes of taking any of the above actions. What are the negative things that can happen if you do any of the above? Think about how likely it is for each of those to happen. Then think about the positive things that can come from taking any of the above actions. Think about the benefits that may arise for the collective good of the team, conference or organisation. Weigh the negative with the positive.

Would you go ahead with reducing the space you occupy, or not?

Checklist

In your journey in letting go of the fear of change through openness, have you:
- ☐ recognised and reflected on your privilege?
- ☐ educated yourself to debunk the myths about DEI?
- ☐ identified your bias buddies?
- ☐ avoided othering others?
- ☐ actively sought out alternative perspectives?
- ☐ taken the time to understand what DEI really means?
- ☐ reflected on the opportunities that DEI creates for you, your team and your company?

Stop-Start-Continue

- -

To become more open and let go of the fear of change, write down in your notebook what you are going to stop doing, start doing and continue doing from now on based on the tools in this chapter.

- -

To let go of our fear of change, we need to be open. This openness enables us to turn the perceived threats of DEI to opportunities, and we can do this by understanding our privilege, debunking the myths, moving from a scarcity mindset to an abundance mindset and by decentering ourselves.

Chapter 5

—

Let go of the fear of getting it wrong with curiosity

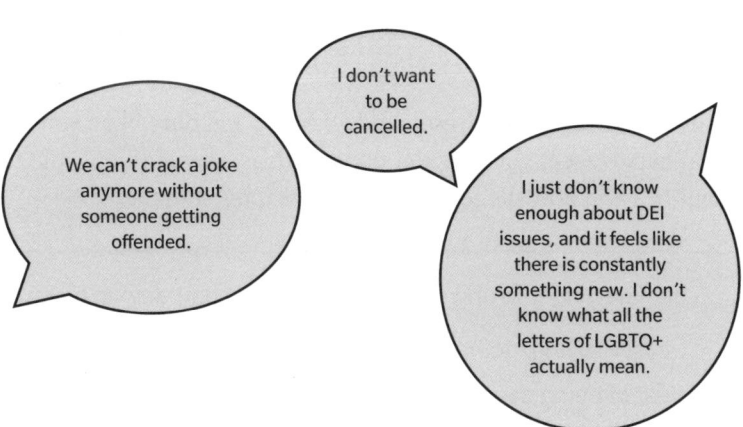

The fear of getting it wrong

- Have you ever found yourself biting your tongue, hesitating to say something to another person, afraid that it may offend them?
- Have you ever felt worried that you may be 'cancelled' for saying and doing the wrong thing, even when you were well-intentioned?
- Have you ever been worried about being labelled a 'racist', 'sexist' or TERF (trans-exclusionary radical feminist) for sharing a concern?
- Have you ever held back from cracking a joke at a meeting, unsure of how people may perceive you?
- Have you ever felt overwhelmed by all the acronyms and vocabulary in DEI?
- Have you ever felt inadequate or insecure, not knowing enough about the topics in DEI?
- Have you ever felt nervous or scared, like you are walking on eggshells, afraid of saying or doing the 'wrong thing'?
- Have you ever hesitated to give feedback to someone from a marginalised group to avoid being seen as prejudiced?
- Have you ever felt hesitant to even engage in a DEI activity out of fear that you may get something wrong?

If any of these questions resonated with you and have been your personal experience, you are not alone. This is how many people feel about DEI and how the fear of 'getting it wrong' shows up.

Fear of getting it wrong encapsulates the accompanying fears:

- Fear of saying/doing the wrong thing.
- Fear of being cancelled.
- Fear of being perceived as incompetent in matters of DEI.
- Fear of having a negative or unintended impact.

- Fear of not knowing enough about the DEI topic.
- Fear of impact of failures or missteps on your (public) image.
- Fear of not knowing the words and phrases.

Do you recognise any of these fears in yourself?

Once we have become aware of this fear, the question is – how do we let go of it? The answer involves addressing the root cause of the fear of getting it wrong – not knowing enough about DEI-related topics and issues. Though it sounds simple enough, to get to the heart of this fear requires curiosity – curiosity to unlearn and learn and to make mistakes. Through curiosity, we expand our understanding about the bias and discrimination around us, which enables us to stop seeing DEI as a threat and, instead, start seeing it as an opportunity for growth and self-development. So, how can we develop this curiosity?

Developing curiosity

Unlearn and learn

'And then there's the fear of incompetence that I don't really know about this [subject area], that I don't really get it, that I will say the wrong thing.'

HR leader

Our organisations reward us for knowing rather than learning. Most of the parameters upon which we are evaluated refer to behaviours that show what we know and how we have applied what we know to achieve our KPIs (key performance indicators) or OKRs (objectives and key results). It is rare to find parameters that reflect what we have learnt.

For those who are leaders, people expect that we have the necessary answers and know-how. This creates an environment where everyone is eager to prove what they know to each other and that what they know is right. When it comes to understanding bias and discrimination, identifying and blocking bias is new to most of us. It's a new muscle we are trying to build. We might be hesitant to let others know we don't know what to do and, instead of admitting that, we try to hide our insecurity. We have been conditioned into believing that not having all the answers is a sign of weakness, but the truth is none of us knows everything. In the words of Harvard Business School professor, Dr Amy Edmondson, 'The simple act of choosing learning over knowing is to recognise that our spontaneous reaction is knowing – we think we're right.'

For most of us, learning about our biases and how to stop them from influencing our words and actions is new. It may sound strange, but learning about our biases begins with unlearning. Throughout our lives, we have learned to have certain views of the world and of other people. There are times when these socially conditioned attitudes harm others and uphold systemic and cultural inequity. Unlearning a lifetime of conditioning is not easy but it is essential to learning new ways and approaches. In unlearning, we are trying to make what is familiar strange. This means questioning all the things that we have taken for granted or accepted as 'just how it is', and questioning our automatic and unconscious behavioural patterns. Think about all the aspects of organisational life in which you have assumed that 'this is just how things have always been done'. In unlearning, we are deleting prior knowledge that has become obsolete[189] or storing knowledge that we do not need now for use at a later time.[190]

When it comes to DEI, the subject matter and vocabulary are new to many of us. One additional challenge is that the terminology and content in the field is constantly evolving and growing. If you have ever felt that it was hard to keep up, you are not alone.

In a recent workshop that I conducted, a participant shared his concern with gender-neutral pronouns. As a British man, he expressed that using the plural pronoun 'they' in a singular form was something that felt strange. He shared that he could hear his English teacher's voice in his head saying that it was 'wrong'. This resonated with me and was an experience I shared. I was educated in the British education system, a system established during colonisation in Singapore, and socially conditioned into what 'proper English' meant. I too had initially struggled with using 'they' in its singular form. I found it hard to come to terms with because of how it would work in a sentence. But then, I attended an event where I heard from a panel of non-binary and gender-fluid people who shared why having gender-neutral pronouns was important to them. It then hit me. This was not about me or my 'proper' use of English. This was about challenging my binary view of the world to create a safe space for others to share their pronouns and for others to self-identify as they wish to. Language and vocabulary evolve, as they always have, and it is important to recognise that we need to adapt to the times we live in; addressing the needs of others to ensure that our language remains not just relevant but inclusive as well. Using inclusive language is an easy way to practise decentring yourself.

Many of us grew up hearing the word 'handicapped'. In the 1990s, there was a push to replace the word 'handicapped' with disabled. This is known as *identity-first language* where the disability is the focus, allowing individuals to own their disability and choose their identity. With this approach, we would say a disabled person or an autistic person. More recently, there has been a push towards *person-first language* that emphasises the person. In this case, we would say a person with disabilities. How a person prefers to be addressed is a personal preference. There is no one way that will be preferred for everyone. It may seem confusing or daunting. What is most important is that we move away from seeing the word 'disabled' as something that is negative and offensive. That means moving away from associating the word 'disabled' with 'unable', 'inspiring' or 'special'. It is important that we use words in a way that avoids negative connotations. This can be extended to the use of phrases like 'this is my blind spot', 'this is my team's handicap' or 'this is lame and dumb'. Such phrases perpetuate the stereotype that disabilities are negative.

This is just one of the challenges with DEI terminology and understanding. Most of us didn't grow up with the vocabulary of diversity and inclusion. We may never have thought about equity outside the financial realm before. We may still be trying to understand what allyship is. To make it even more challenging, most of the terms used in DEI emerged from English-speaking contexts and cannot be translated easily into other languages. Finding a one-to-one translation can be difficult. If you speak a language other than English, take a moment to think about how you would translate DEI-related words and phrases.

Language is one aspect; broader societal norms and issues are another. DEI is understood differently in different cultural contexts and may have a different focus. While in the USA, DEI is often centred on addressing racial inequity, in Japan, the focus is likely to be discrimination based on gender and age. In India, the focus is likely addressing caste, gender and religious inequities. The acts of discrimination and inequity that DEI aims to address is highly contextual, and a one-size-fits-all approach simply won't work. This makes it especially challenging when working with DEI across global contexts, languages and culture. When I work with companies based in Italy, France, Denmark, India and Singapore, one of my priorities is to explore what these words mean in local languages and in local contexts. This involves explaining what a term like allyship means and then allowing time for discussion on how allyship shows up in the local context. That helps build understanding and deeper meaning of terms rather than adopting them from another context. This is what I call the glocal (global-local) approach to DEI.[191]

Remember, it is about unlearning and learning. We must seek to unlearn and learn what we know or think we know about others and DEI. How can we do that?

Educate yourself and seek help

When I moved to Copenhagen in 2014, no one in my immediate circle of colleagues, friends and family were openly part of the LGBTQ+ community. Until then, I had lived in a part of the world where it was illegal to be part of the LGBTQ+ community. While I was aware of the challenges faced by the community through my research, I didn't have any first-hand interactions with people from that community. Everything I knew was theoretical rather than based on personal narratives. A few months after moving to Denmark, I attended an event at the Copenhagen Business School during which a transwoman shared her experiences of discrimination in Denmark. Hearing her personal experiences touched something inside of me and I spent time educating myself about the experiences of those who identify as being part of the LGBTQ+ community. I had to learn what each letter in LGBTQ+ represents and understand how varied the experiences of those who identify that way are in different parts of the world. Then I had to unlearn the social conditioning and biases that had, until that point in time, influenced my social and cultural context. Through my work, I have met many inspiring members of the LGBTQ+ community who have been colleagues and mentors as I continue to unlearn and learn.

If we want to make our workplaces more inclusive, we must first understand that our experiences of discrimination are not shared and, in order to understand that, we must educate ourselves. It is our responsibility to unlearn our pre-held beliefs, stereotypes and prejudices. Educating ourselves also involves challenging our pre-held beliefs and assumptions about what is good practice in our organisations. I often hear from leaders that they became aware of stereotypes, prejudices and discrimination when their daughter reached working age or when their child came out as gay or lesbian or when someone close to them became disabled in an accident. We should not need someone in our close personal lives to be a part of a marginalised group to feel the need to educate ourselves on how to make our workplaces more inclusive.

Many business best practices emanate from a Global North and colonial perspective. We superimpose these practices, including systems, structures, policies and culture on others, assuming that it is the 'better way'. These practices include what we consider to be effective organisational structures, workplace cultures and leadership behaviours. By implementing these structures without regard for cultural context, we ignore indigenous practices that are often better suited for local contexts. Educating ourselves through cross-cultural awareness to adopt a glocal (global-local) approach is key, while also incorporating indigenous ways of knowing, being, doing and relating into organisational, cultural and social structures; a process known as indigenisation. This is essential for people from diverse and Global South backgrounds to feel included – to be seen, valued and heard – and for organisational effectiveness in various cultural contexts. We have been so conditioned by the Global North's dominant cultural norms that were and are forced upon us, that we assume that these cultural norms are 'better' for all when in fact they are not. We need to decolonise what we know, that is what we have always been told is the better or right way of doing things, and the best way to do that is to widen our understanding. Sometimes, I hear comments that decolonisation is an effort to erase the identity and history of those who come from countries who were colonisers. It isn't. Decolonisation is an effort to understand history in its fullness, and its impact on our current power structures and systemic/institutional bias so that we can take actions to level the playing field.

Educating ourselves – learning – is a constant process. In the words of the nineteenth century US writer Mary Roberts Reinhart: 'When knowledge comes in the door, fear and superstition fly out.' When I find gaps in my own understanding that hold me back from engaging in DEI conversation, I make a conscious effort to find out more to fill the gap. In today's information age, there are plenty of resources out there to help us satisfy our curiosity by educating ourselves. It's important to note that learning does not mean asking people from marginalised groups to share or explain their life experiences. Instead, we can educate ourselves by reading books, listening to an audiobook or podcast, or reading one of many articles out there. We can follow people on social media who have made it their life's work to educate us to be inclusive. We can attend events by speakers from a different background and be curious about their life stories and experiences. Over the past few years, I have been reading books, listening to podcasts and engaging in conversations to help me gain a deeper understanding of colonisation, slavery and neocolonialism in different parts of the world to broaden and deepen my own understanding of the experiences of people of colour and the influence of these systems of oppression on current inequity. I am reminded of the words of Marie Curie, 'Nothing in life is to be feared. It is only to be understood.'

When we feel that we don't know enough about a topic when engaging on it with others, we may feel anxious or fearful, which, in turn, may keep us from engaging. We can seek help by saying the following:

- 'I would like to know more about this topic, can you point me in the right direction for some articles, podcasts and authors whose content I can read/listen to?'

- 'Could you tell me more about this? It is not a topic I know a lot about and would love to know more.'

- 'I'm going to take some time to understand more about this before we engage on it. Please give me some time to do my own research and then we can have a conversation about it.'

Once you have made the effort to educate yourself, take time to deeply reflect on what you have read/listened to. Dwell on it and go deep. Allow the know-how to be internalised. That's when it has the potential to change our attitudes and behaviours.

 # DEI topics I want to know more about

What are the DEI topics I want to know more about? It could be about the discrimination a particular marginalised group experiences or the history behind the DEI challenges we experience today. Write them down in your notebook.

Take time to understand the deeper meaning of words and terms

Since 2019, there has been an uptake of the use of the word 'woke' as an insult by opponents of DEI efforts. It is often used to mock 'over righteous liberalism'. If we looked at the media's coverage and usage of the word woke as an insult, we might walk away thinking that it means 'following an intolerant and moralising ideology'.[192] But what does woke actually mean?

Woke is an adjective derived from African American Vernacular English (AAVE). Its original meaning was associated with an alertness to racial prejudice and discrimination. Today, it's usually defined as being aware and attentive of societal issues, especially social justice and race.[193] That's certainly not the meaning that is being used by 'anti-woke' proponents. It is easy for people to hurl words and phrases like 'anti-woke' and 'anti-DEI' but I wonder how many people would be willing to say that they are anti-fairness, anti-uniqueness and anti-belonging? How many people would openly declare that they are anti-social justice? Unlearning and learning means taking the time to understand the meaning of the words that are associated with DEI as the vocabulary is relatively new to many of us and it is likely that our understanding may be inaccurate.

Keep in mind that DEI-related language can also be understood differently in different cultural contexts. What this means is that someone using a word or phrase may not have intended to have used it as an offensive comment, but rather that they may not have understood its meaning. This arises more frequently with people speaking English as a second or third language. In such situations, give the benefit of doubt. Make an effort to try and find out what was meant rather than assuming that it was used as you understood it. Once you have engaged in understanding how the person meant it, then engage in a conversation about how the use of that word or phrase is discriminatory to a particular group. Use this as an opportunity to help the other person learn.

Learning and unlearning is the first step in developing curiosity – but we can't stop there. We then need to take the necessary actions to make change happen.

Be inclusive in your communication

'I think there are a lot of bad actors that have contributed to a lot of bullying and cancelling. If you say a word wrong, or if you use something incorrectly, people have been humiliated in public. People have been shamed into a lot of guilt.'

DEI expert

Exclusionary or non-inclusive communication, also known as microaggressions, are pervasive. According to a 2023 Women in the Workplace report, women experience microaggressions at a significantly higher rate than men.[194] Women are twice as likely as men to be mistaken for someone junior and hear comments on their emotional state, and two and a half times as likely to face comments about their appearance. For women with traditionally marginalised identities, the prevalence of microaggressions increases even more. Asian and black women are seven times more likely than white women to be confused with someone of the same race and ethnicity. LGBTQ+ women are six and a half times more likely to face comments about their appearance than men. Women with disabilities are two and half times more likely to have their judgement questioned, four times more likely to face comments on their emotional state and six times more likely to face a comment about their appearance than men.

Coined by Dr Chester Pierce in the 1970s, microaggressions are everyday acts of discrimination, often rooted in bias and consist of statements, actions or incidents that are considered to be an instance of indirect, subtle or unintentional discrimination against members of a marginalised group. Research shows us that subtle discrimination has as much of a negative impact on our psychological and physical health, as well as work-related behaviours, as overt discrimination.[195] Microaggressions have a cumulative and pervasive effect on those who experience them, and negatively impact psychological well-being, causing anger, shock and shame.[196] They also deplete energy and lead to lower productivity and problem-solving capability. [197]

The term has been criticised recently for failing to fully capture the extent of the negative impact. 'Micro' suggests that the damage is not as serious when, in fact, it is.[198] Microaggressions are like a quiet disease, silently eating away at inclusion. They create a lowered sense of psychological well-being[199] and deplete energy and work productivity. While they may seem small, the effect is cumulative. In an effort to move away from the use of the term 'micro' and its limitations, I refer to exclusionary communication as 'termite biases' in my book *The Art of Active Allyship*. Termites do more damage to our economy than any other pest, but you don't even know they are there until significant damage has been done, much like microaggressions. What this exclusionary communication does is to make people feel 'othered'.

Exclusionary communication can take many forms: a casual comment, a joke, a compliment or even a well-intentioned remark. It also includes how we provide feedback to others. Studies show that women and non-white employees receive as much as 20% less feedback and lower quality or less actionable feedback than men and white employees.[200] Why does this disparity exist? Dr David A. Thomas calls this 'protective hesitation'.[201] It's when 'a leader fails to give constructive criticism to an employee out of fear of being perceived as racist, sexist, homophobic, or any other prejudice' to avoid the risk of getting it wrong or ruining your self-image.[202]

Below are some other common examples of exclusionary communication. Do you recognise them? Would you add some to the list?

Competency-related exclusionary communication:

These non-inclusive behaviours reflect the low expectations of the abilities of a person, surprise when they demonstrate competency or beliefs that they are 'affirmative action' of 'quota' or 'token' hires.

'Congrats on your new role. You are so fortunate to be a woman, there are so many opportunities for you.'

'She is an accidental CEO. She hasn't had a conventional career pathway to the top. I wonder if she has what it takes to actually be CEO.'

'Sorry, can you get me a cup of coffee please' (said to a female CEO).

'All they want are women. You must be in great demand – as a brown woman. Lucky you!'

'They'll probably pick you as the leader cause you're black.'

'You're good at this for a woman.'

'I'm so proud of Ana, she took it like a man.'

'Are you sure you can still handle this project since you are having a baby?'

'You must be having some serious pregnancy brain today!'

'She gets too emotional. Not leadership material.'

'She/he is not a "good fit".'

'Are you sure you can do that with your disability?'

'Wow, you are so inspiring being able to do all this despite your disability. I could never do that.'

'You're too young to understand.'

'You haven't experienced enough of the world to know.'

'Aren't you too old to know this?'

'Are you sure about this? Maybe we should verify it with Tom. He has a lot more experience than you do.'

Communication-related exclusionary communication:

These non-inclusive behaviours reflect the surprise at the communication capabilities of a person, the low respect for their opinion and view and stereotyping a person to be better at non-promotable tasks that are hard to say no to.

'You are so good at taking notes and organising events. Can you please do this for the team?'

'I didn't expect you to speak English so well!'

'You sound white.'

'How did you get rid of your accent?'

'Oh my, I love your accent.'

'Ugh, I can't stand listening to them. They just sound so uneducated.'

'Do you have to be that aggressive when making your point?'

'You really should smile more often.'

'How did you learn to speak English so well?'

'She's always nagging the team.'

'She could smile instead of the resting bitch face.'

Interrupting or speaking over a person in meetings.

Taking credit for someone else's ideas.

Assuming women are responsible for office housework.

Dismissing a person's ideas or contributions without valid reasons.

Using language that is subtly demeaning or patronising towards women by calling them dear, girl or sweetheart or towards a black man by calling him a 'boy'.

Appearance/identity-related exclusionary communication:

These non-inclusive behaviours reflect the surprise that someone of a particular identity and who looks a particular way is capable or different from what the expectations of someone of that group are.

'Always having blonde moments, that one.'

'Get one of the girls to do it.'

'She needs to grow a pair.'

'Why do you care so much?! You're on your way out on maternity leave anyway!'

'You're so young to be in such a senior role. I thought you were the intern.'

'Where are you actually from?'

'Is that really what you would wear to work in your home country?'

'Wow, your hair is so big today. Maybe you shouldn't take the client meeting, we don't want them thinking we are unprofessional.'

'You all look the same.'

'You are so exotic.'

'Yeah, but you're not black black.'

Referring to a white person as a 'man' or 'woman' but someone from a non-white background by an adjective like 'Indian', 'Asian' or 'Latina'.

'You're not like other Muslim people.'

'Your name is too hard to pronounce, do you have a short form?'

'You're really pretty for someone so dark.'

'When I see you, I don't see colour.'

'Oh you're black! Your name suggested that you were white.'

'Are you fasting for Ramadan? We might need to call an ambulance.'

'I find you intimidating.' (Black female employees being told that by colleagues.)

'Go back to where you came from.'

'Wow, you're trans? You look like a real woman.'

'You're not gay, you could easily pass as a straight man.'

'You're too short, blonde and petite to be a CEO.'

'Your voice isn't deep enough to be a leader. People won't listen to you.'

'You're leaving early, is your wife on holiday?'

'You look lovely and I love what you are wearing.'

'Pale, male and stale.'

What can we do to be more inclusive in our communication?

Check your language

Checking our choice of words and phrases is an important aspect of unlearning and learning. A 2024 article in *The Times* declared the 'Death of the chairman: City switching to more inclusive "chairs"' highlighting the move among many FTSE100 companies preferring gender-neutral titles.[203]

Think about the words and phrases that you use that may reflect societal stereotypes and prejudices and that may 'other' someone. Are there any that come to your mind? Questioning the language that we use is a great place to start. If you have discussions about the language we use, you may find that some members of marginalised communities may not find certain words discriminatory, while others may. It could be that they have been socially conditioned into not recognising the bias at play or just accepting things as they are. When in doubt, it is always better to use inclusive language.

You could consider flipping words around to disrupt our patterns that reinforce norms that give privilege and power to some groups more than others. For example, try saying 'hers and his' instead of 'his and hers'. Try and greet the brown or black person first, then white people, in a meeting. Try not to default to a builder, lawyer or doctor being a 'he'. You could also consider addressing your email to the person who is from a marginalised group first. While these might seem like small acts individually, their cumulative impact is significant in challenging existing norms. Don't underestimate the power of these 'micro' acts.

 # Swapping words and phrases

Below are some examples of biased language for you to think about in the English language. If you aren't sure why one of the words or phrases below is biased or discriminatory, look it up. You may be surprised by the answer you get. Add to this list or write down words and phrases in your own spoken languages other than English. What would you swap them with to make them more inclusive?

Instead of . . .	Try . . .
Hey guys	*For example:* 'Hey folks' or 'Hey everyone'
Good morning ladies and gentlemen	
Chairman/policeman/fireman	
Manpower/two-man job/middleman	
Don't cry like a girl	
Homosexual/transexual/transvestite	
Blacklist/blackmark/blackmail/black sheep	
Savage/barbaric	
I'm a slave to my work	
Chop-chop	
Gramps/Grandma, OK boomer, snowflake/trophy generation	
Grandfather clause/grandfather policy	
Blindspot/blindsided/blind leading the blind	
This is lame/dumb/crazy	
Don't be a spaz/retarded/idiot/insane/psycho	
This is our team's handicap	
Tone deaf	
The work has paralysed/crippled me	

Engage inclusively

Think about leaving every space you are in more inclusive than when you entered it. In the words of Peter Drucker, the founder of modern management, 'Our mission on earth is to make a positive difference.'

To communicate inclusively:

- *Avoid jargon and complex language.*
  Go back to the basics of what DEI actually means when engaging on the topic. Avoid using language and jargon that makes it complex both for you and for others and creates opportunities for misunderstanding and misinterpretation. Keep it simple and grounded in the core principles of what DEI is about – uniqueness, fairness and belonging.

- *Make an effort with people's names.*
  Our names reflect our identity, culture and background. They are important to us so make a genuine effort to spell and pronounce another person's name in emails, text messages and in conversations the way that they would spell and pronounce it. Unfortunately, technology is not going to help us with this. Did you know that 41% of children's names in the UK are considered to be a typo and are autocorrected?[204]

Of course, we may not always know how to pronounce or spell everyone's names, so respectfully ask the person how they would pronounce or spell their name, and make an effort to try to get it right. You may not get the pronunciation right the first time or the second, but keep trying until you do. And referring to my own experience that I shared at the start of the book, avoid referring to people whose names are less familiar to you with just a single letter. I certainly don't want to be known as 'P' especially when others' names are spelt/said in full. My name, Poornima, means full moon. I was born on a full moon day and my paternal grandmother suggested the name since a full moon is regarded as being an auspicious day of positive energy and vibrancy in Indian mythology and culture. My name is a reminder to me and those around me of my rich heritage, the colour of my skin, my culture, my background, my family and, in all this – my identity. Spelling and pronouncing people's names is a simple way to show respect and inclusion of others' identity.

- *Use flip questions and scenarios.*
  When tempted to ask a question to someone that may be discriminatory, sense check by asking yourself a flip question – would you ask that question to a man, or to a white woman, or to an able-bodied person? If not, don't ask that question. Imagine this: a heterosexual couple have both returned from maternity leave. What do we as colleagues/bosses say to one party versus the other? Are we saying the same thing? And if not, why?

- *Ask open-ended questions.*
  My favourite phrase that I use is 'tell me about yourself'. It allows the other person to control the narrative and what they feel safe to share with us. Whatever their response is, believe it and avoid asking follow-on questions that reflect the stereotypes in your mind about who they 'should be' or 'should not be'.

- *Avoid taking credit for someone else's ideas and interrupting others.*
  If it should happen, remember to redirect the stolen credit back to the person who first made a suggestion or offered an idea, and disrupt the interruption by recreating the space for the person who was interrupted to complete what they were saying.

- *Redirect focus from intention to impact.*
  There is a big difference between intention and impact. We often think that our intentions are good enough. For example, we may say, 'But I didn't mean it that way.' While you may have had good intentions, remember that the impact that you have matters. If harm is caused, then we need to take ownership and take accountability.

Engage in intelligent failures

'I went to this diversity event. There was a younger black woman who said something. I spoke up right after her, and responded to what she said – added on or critiqued it. I was shouted down by an older black woman who told me, "Here's a white woman breaking in and rewording the same stuff." I didn't feel that I had done that. But you know she just shattered me down publicly. That was pretty intimidating. I didn't want to go back into the conference. I felt bad. I thought – did I really take away her words? I thought I was critiquing what she said. I thought that was allowed, but she interpreted it through a power lens. And then I was in doubt. Did I actually do that or not do that? I don't think that I did that. I thought I was being unjustly judged but I wasn't sure. It was a pretty horrible experience. I was younger then. I was in my late twenties. It was pretty intense. Being called a racist at a public event felt pretty bad.'

HR leader

When it comes to DEI, many of us fear getting it wrong. We are afraid of saying the wrong thing, using the wrong terminology, being biased or being perceived to be prejudiced. We might be afraid of being ostracised, boycotted, shunned, fired or assaulted because of what we said or did. This extends to a fear of implementing DEI initiatives, not knowing if we are doing it right and scared that by trying to be inclusive to one group we will end up excluding another. This occurs from an incorrect understanding that DEI is a marginalised community issue – rather than a strategic and organisational one. This is where the challenge at an organisational level lies – leaders are fearful of making broad systemic change. What if things don't work out? Changing something that appears to be working to something that doesn't is taking a big risk.

It is important to remember that we are all learning along the way. There will be times we get it right and other times when we don't but we cannot let fear of failing hold us back from engaging in DEI initiatives.

A few years ago, I was having dinner with my family when my then 11-year-old son, Rohan, was sharing that a guest speaker from Google had given a presentation at school that day. Without pausing for a moment, I asked, 'Was he a dad at school?' As the words rolled off my tongue, I recognised my bias. I was hoping no one at the table noticed but my family is well-trained. My husband rolled his eyes and my son jumped up, pointing it out to me: 'Mom, that was so biased of you . . . and it was a woman!' The somewhat embarrassing part is that I had a very clear image in my head of what the person from Google talking about data looked like. In my mind, he was an Indian man. I could describe exactly what I imagined him to look like, sound like and could even tell you about his likely life story. There I was, my bias laid out on the dinner table for all to see. Having my bias pointed out to me made me feel ashamed. After all, this is what I do for a living. I had conducted a bias awareness training for a client just that morning. While I am happy my son caught the bias in my comment, it was still uncomfortable. I had to accept the vulnerability of admitting the mistake and sit with it. My response to him was: 'Good catch, sweetheart, good catch.'

During a DEI panel discussion, a senior leader of a company shared a biased comment she had made to her entire team. During an end-of-year online meeting in 2021, she signed off by wishing everyone on the call 'Merry Christmas'. Her husband, who had been in the other room listening in – the unwanted side effects of working from home, perhaps – came over and asked her if the session went well. This senior leader energetically responded by highlighting how thrilled she was to end the year on such a high note. He then asked: 'You wished everyone Merry Christmas. Do you think everyone on the call celebrates Christmas?' To the large audience of colleagues gathered at that panel session, she expressed the embarrassment she felt at the idea that she had said something that favoured one group over another. Not only did she have to sit with the discomfort of possibly offending her colleagues, but also the uncomfortable feeling of having her husband point it out to her. Her response? 'Aagh, that was a rookie mistake. Of course not. I should have said "Happy Holidays!"'

We will make mistakes. Even those of us who work with DEI will make mistakes. What if we could reframe the way we see these moments of mistakes as opportunities for learning and growth? What if we are curious enough to do and see things differently, and start seeing these moments when we 'get it wrong' as intelligent failures?

The concept of intelligent failure was developed by Harvard Business School professor, Dr Amy Edmondson. In her book, *Right Kind of Wrong*, Professor Edmondson challenges us to rethink how we look at failure.[205] We used to think failure was a negative issue and then we pivoted to looking at failure as desirable, that we must 'fail fast, fail often'. In her book, Professor Edmondson argues that neither extremes enable us to distinguish between good failures and bad ones. She suggests that there are three forms of failure – complex, basic and intelligent failures. These vary in terms of increasing uncertainty and reduced preventability, meaning that basic failures are those that have the least uncertainty and the greatest chance of being preventable, while intelligent failures have the greatest uncertainty and lowest preventability. Complex failures occur in familiar settings but where multiple factors interact in unexpected and uncontrollable ways and are perhaps the least relevant in the DEI space.

Basic failures are usually caused by human error which results in an undesired outcome – we made a mistake. Many of our daily mistakes in the busyness of our day are basic failures. Some of our DEI efforts may constitute basic failures when, because of inattention, assumptions, overconfidence and neglect, we end up getting it wrong.[206] For example, misspelling someone's name or referring to someone with their incorrect pronouns even though you knew what their pronouns were. My experience with my son or the senior leader wishing people Merry Christmas are examples of basic failures. Our assumptions and neglect led us to act in a way that was discriminatory.

Intelligent failures happen in new territory, where the context presents a credible opportunity to advance a desired goal, when it is informed by available knowledge and when the failure is as small as it can be to provide valuable insights. For intelligent failures to take place, psychological safety is essential. Professor Edmondson defines psychological safety as 'a shared belief held by members of a team that the team is safe for interpersonal risk taking'[207] and this psychological safety is essential for individuals and teams to take risks and engage in intelligent failures.

For most people in organisations, DEI efforts to address systemic and cultural bias is new terrain or relatively new terrain. While DEI initiatives have been around for a while, it is only more recently that organisations have begun to make systemic and cultural change. This includes embedding bias blockers and equity measures across the entire employee life cycle, nurturing psychological safety to address bias and discrimination, implementing inclusive design principles in product and service development and ensuring inclusive marketing campaigns.

The additional efforts and commitment is why there is backlash and resistance. There is more at stake, and the fear of getting it wrong is prevalent. Yet, such transformational DEI initiatives present a definite opportunity to move things forward towards greater inclusion, diversity and equity in our workplaces, and are grounded in robust evidence, research and know-how. Experimenting in these efforts should be seen as opportunities for intelligent failures that provide opportunities for growth and progress.

The term 'growth mindset' was made famous by Carol Dweck in her book, *Mindset – The New Psychology of Success* in which she differentiates between having a growth mindset and a fixed mindset. Individuals who believe that their talents can be developed through hard work, good strategies and input from others have a growth mindset. On the other hand, those who believe that their talents are innate gifts have a fixed mindset. According to Dweck: 'They [people with a growth mindset] tend to achieve more than those with a more fixed mindset . . . When entire companies embrace a growth mindset, their employees report feeling far more empowered and committed; they also receive greater organisational support for collaboration and innovation.'[208]

'How do I know when it's right to step in as an ally?' It is one of the questions I get asked frequently. What if we get it wrong and step in when the other person wanted to address the discrimination themselves? What if in doing so we inadvertently take away their agency and voice? What if it comes across as saviourism? What if the person I am trying to support gets upset and angry with me? What if it negatively affects my relationship with them? In trying to be an ally, what if I harm the very person I wanted to support? This is a challenging situation that can occur frequently – should I step in or not?

This is an excellent opportunity to engage in an intelligent failure. It might be new territory in the sense that being an ally is maybe new to you, it has the opportunity to address discrimination and nurture inclusion, you have the know-how and, in the bigger scheme of things, the failure is small. What is the worst thing that can happen? The person you were trying to support is upset with you? That is a risk worth taking for a possible positive outcome of addressing the discrimination at play.

So, how do you decide if you should act or not? First, read the situation and feel the vibe in the room. Observe the person being discriminated against for clues on how they are feeling and if they will address the discrimination themselves. In the absence of clear cues that your allyship is not needed, step in as an ally. Don't let fear of failure hold you back from being an ally. Ask yourself if you would rather be a bystander and allow that discrimination to continue or be told off for taking someone's voice? Is it better to be a potentially unnecessary ally than a bystander who missed the moment? Even if allyship was not needed, it sends a message to everyone that it's a normal everyday thing to look out for each other and may encourage them to demonstrate the same behaviour. If it turns out that you overstepped in your actions, apologise to the person and use the opportunity to engage in a dialogue on what you could have done differently.

Accept that you will make mistakes. Instead of focusing on getting it right all the time – and in turn avoiding engagement – focus on using every interaction as an opportunity to learn from an intelligent failure. Be curious and ask yourself the following questions:

- What can I learn from this?
- How can I change the words I am using to be more inclusive?
- What words, language or topics do I need to learn more about?

In engaging with DEI, view your efforts as an experiment, even if things don't quite go as you hoped. Learn what worked, what did not and what needs to be done differently the next time to achieve positive outcomes. Remember, if you get it wrong, it does not mean you are not a good person or leader. Don't see it as a blow to your ego but instead as a growth opportunity to learn and do it better. Then transform your intelligent failure into success.

Checklist

In your journey in letting go of the fear of getting it wrong through curiosity, have you:
- ☐ educated yourself on DEI topics, making an effort to go deeper in your understanding?
- ☐ made an effort to ensure that the words and phrases that you use are inclusive?
- ☐ avoided using jargon and complex language when discussing DEI?
- ☐ used flip questions and scenarios to check yourself?
- ☐ asked open-ended questions when interacting with others?
- ☐ redirected stolen credit back to the person who first made a suggestion or offered an idea?
- ☐ disrupted interruptions in meetings by recreating the space for the person who was interrupted to complete what they were saying?
- ☐ redirected your focus away from intention to the impact of your actions?

➤

☐ engaged in intelligent failures, focusing on what you unlearned and learnt?

 # Stop-Start-Continue

To become more curious and let go of the fear of getting it wrong, write down in your notebook what you are going to stop doing, start doing and continue doing from now on based on the tools in this chapter.

To let go of our fear of getting it wrong, we need to have curiosity. This curiosity enables us to turn the perceived threats of DEI into opportunities, and we can do this by unlearning and learning, being inclusive in our communication and engaging in intelligent failures.

Chapter 6

Let go of the fear of discomfort with vulnerability

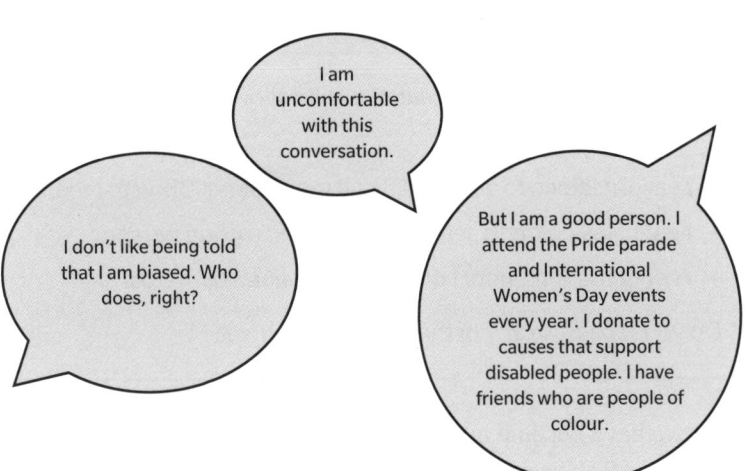

Fear of discomfort

Have you ever felt discomfort when someone addresses a bias or act of discrimination?

Have you ever been hesitant to attend an Employee Resource Group (ERG) event because you are part of the 'majority' and may feel uncomfortable hearing the stories of discrimination?

No one wants to be in a conversation where they feel uncomfortable.

No one wants to be in a conversation where they feel guilt or shame.

No one wants to be in a conversation where they are made to feel like they are 'bad'.

Even the possibility of discomfort often keeps us away from engaging in DEI initiatives. We may feel exposed when our biases are pointed out, or even persecuted. We may feel like we are not good people because of our biased actions or words. We may feel rejected by champions of DEI because we said or did something that was biased, even though we believe in what DEI stands for.

This fear of discomfort holds us back from engaging in DEI efforts.

Fear of discomfort encapsulates the following accompanying fears:

- Fear of needing to discuss difficult topics about DEI with others.
- Fear of losing one's self-image of being a good person.
- Fear of the discomfort of addressing one's own bias.

Do you recognise any of these fears in yourself?

Once we have become aware of this fear, the question is – how do we let go of it? The answer involves addressing the root cause of the fear of discomfort – knowing that we are biased like everyone else. To acknowledge the biases in ourselves requires vulnerability. It is not easy to come to terms with the fact that we are all biased and to discuss this with others. We need to allow ourselves the grace and space to sit with the discomfort that comes from examining our biases, knowing that it is in these moments of discomfort that the desire to make change happen is born. In making space for vulnerability, we become comfortable with the discomfort and, in doing so, we move away from seeing DEI as a threat, and instead start seeing it as an opportunity for making progress. Vulnerability is something that can be developed in ourselves. The question is, how?

Developing vulnerability

Get comfortable with discomfort

It is likely that, when we think of 'bias' we have an image in our mind. Perhaps it is of someone overtly racist wearing a robe and white hat, or someone who engages in blatant sexism. We probably associate being biased with extreme behaviour and negativity. We equate being biased with being 'bad'. Remember, however, that everyone is biased. We all rely on those mental shortcuts to help us categorise information. Our biases – consciously or unconsciously – influence our words, actions, and decisions. And yet, we often feel ashamed and guilty of being biased. Most of us want to be seen as being fair and rational, when in reality, many of us are not.

Because we associate 'bias' with 'bad', we get uncomfortable when we realise we hold biases against others or when our biases are pointed out to us. This discomfort holds us back. It stops us from becoming aware of our biases, which is the only way we can block their influence on how we engage with others and make decisions. We may get uncomfortable when we realise our privilege or begin to recognise how many of the systems, structures and culture around us are biased to favour us and not others. We may get uncomfortable when our non-inclusive behaviours are pointed out or questioned.

Discomfort, especially in the context of DEI, is inevitable. The journey towards embracing equity and inclusion will involve many moments of discomfort. Yet, the discomfort is natural, expected and shows your commitment to this process. It is in this state of discomfort that we can learn the most about ourselves and how we interact with others. Getting uncomfortable and wriggling in your seat are exactly where you should be.

How do we tend to respond to this discomfort? According to Dr Robert Livingston, Harvard social psychologist, we engage in channel switching, which he defines as 'an effort – intentional or inadvertent – to divert a conversation about race or racism (typically, anti-black racism) to a topic that is more palatable or personally relevant to the individual attempting to shift the focus – say, to women's rights or diversity of thought, for example.'[209] Livingston argues that as the backlash against DEI has increased, so has channel switching. This channel switching reflects our discomfort with discussing certain topics, in this case racism, and redirects it to topics that are more comfortable or relevant to us personally.

What if we reframed how we looked at discomfort? After all, it is in these moments of discomfort that trust is formed, and trust is fundamental to human interactions. Without trust, our interactions with each other are plagued with discomfort. But here is the thing – we are most comfortable trusting the people who are like or similar to us. Trusting people who are different from us and beyond our closest circle of friends and colleagues is often uncomfortable. To nurture inclusion, we have to embrace the discomfort we feel and have difficult conversations about our biases and the discrimination around us. This discomfort is the very thing that will help us to build trust with people beyond our closest circles. If we begin to view the discomfort we experience when engaging in DEI as a way to gain trust, then that discomfort has positive value. What if we become comfortable with the discomfort so that we can be more inclusive?

If the idea of being comfortable in our discomfort as a means to fostering inclusiveness intrigues you, you might be wondering how that would work. Below are a set of tools to help us all get comfortable with the discomfort that comes from unpacking our biases.

Recognise and acknowledge the discomfort

Most of us will find every means to remove ourselves from uncomfortable situations or change the circumstances to move to a state of comfort. We are creatures of habit and routine who enjoy staying in our comfort zone. While there is nothing wrong with habits and routines, staying in our comfort zone for too long can dull our sensitivities and, as we get on with the daily grind, we may stop noticing things around us. When we have new experiences – such as engaging with people from different backgrounds or learning about a new DEI topic – our body creates new neural pathways that alter existing ones to adapt to new experiences, learn new information and create new memories.[210] This neuroplasticity is crucial to developing new and inclusive behaviours based on these new experiences. Most of us have probably found ourselves relying on our 'gut' to help us in making decisions at some point. When deciding which candidate to hire or which direction to take on a project, you may have relied on your 'gut feeling'. While the gut is increasingly referred to as our 'second brain', our gut finds ways to keep us comfortable. So, challenge your gut. In fact, go one step further and interrogate your gut. Ask your gut questions about why it feels that a particular decision should be taken. Keep digging deeper with why and how questions until you are sure that you have made every effort to block bias from the decision-making process, and that you are not simply relying on a 'gut feeling'. In his book, *Linchpin: Are You Indispensable*, Seth Godin wrote, 'Discomfort brings engagement and change.' To change ourselves and enable change around us towards being more inclusive, equitable and open to diversity, we need to first recognise and acknowledge the discomfort that arises when engaging in DEI.

Resist the temptation to play discrimination Olympics

When someone shares their experiences of bias and discrimination, it might feel important to offer our own experiences of discrimination or share someone else's, especially if we consider it more severe. We tend to do this because of the discomfort we feel. When we compare stories of bias or discrimination – 'my discrimination is more (or less) valid than yours' – we end up playing discrimination Olympics. How an individual internalises discrimination is personal. One may brush off a bias or act of discrimination, while another can feel it deeply. Comparing the severity of discrimination from our personal yardstick is not just inaccurate, it is inappropriate.

Why do we engage in such a response? Hearing someone's experiences may trigger a sense of shame or guilt in us. This shame or guilt may arise because we may have never experienced discrimination or maybe we have engaged in a similar action, and we have now become aware of the harm it causes. This shame and guilt are distractions that keep us from taking accountability for our own imperfections. To avoid accountability and to reduce discomfort in ourselves, we share our own experiences in the hope of showing the other person that discrimination is everywhere. We might share the experience of others to illustrate that even privileged people experience discrimination. I was recently having a conversation with a white woman who responded to the discussion on racism that black and brown people experience with, 'I have also experienced discrimination as a white woman.' We might assume that such a statement will provide solace. This is far from reality. We end up discounting or gaslighting the experience of others to ease our discomfort.

Centre the discomfort of others

If DEI makes you uncomfortable, try to consider how someone from a marginalised group feels in situations where they are discriminated against. It may be only recently that you thought about your race and skin colour or sexual orientation. For others, especially those from underrepresented or marginalised groups, they must consider those factors all the time, and even in the moments when they are not thinking about their race and skin colour or sexual orientation, all too often they are reminded by others of the privilege they don't have. Imagine that discomfort every time you feel discomfort. Taking a moment to think about others may help put the discomfort into perspective.

Seek out personal narratives

We are often uncomfortable with things that are unfamiliar to us. When we hear someone share their experiences of discrimination – whether it was as a result of our actions or not – we might feel uncomfortable and avoid further conversation or play discrimination Olympics. One of the ways to get comfortable with the discomfort is to get more familiar with how others experience our workplaces. To do that, we have to actively seek out diverse personal narratives. This does not mean asking people from marginalised groups to share their experiences of discrimination. This means reading or listening to content already available. There are plenty of books, articles or podcasts that can help us get familiar with the experiences of black, LGBTQ+ or disabled people. When we are more familiar, the next time someone raises their experience of discrimination, we can sit with the discomfort and engage in a conversation.

Engaging for progress

Pause before reacting

We don't pause enough. We live in a world where we are rewarded for thinking on our feet and having a quick comeback. When we don't take a moment to pause, we tend to respond reactively rather than intentionally. Hitting pause is especially important when we receive feedback on bias. We may think reactively: I'm not biased, they're wrong! What makes them think they can correct my bias? They are so biased themselves! I'm a good person, how can someone say I am biased?

When we come face to face with moments of discomfort when our bias is pointed out or when engaging on DEI topics, pause before reacting and ask yourself the following:

- Am I seeing this through the perspective of the other person?
- Why is this triggering for me? Why is it affecting me so much? What is it triggering in me? Am I taking this personally, as an attack on me being a 'bad' person?

What to do when bias is pointed out

One of the most uncomfortable situations to be in is when our own bias or act of discrimination is pointed out. It is very likely that we respond with defensiveness: 'But I am a good person'; avoidance: 'This is making me uncomfortable, please stop'; or even leaving the conversation: 'This is too much for me'.

Instead of reacting that way, how can we engage in a conversation that is an opportunity for learning and growth? Remember, the discomfort is inevitable. Instead, we need to learn to leverage it to do better. Below are some good practices.

- Listen more intently and limit interruptions. Practise active and intentional listening to understand rather than to respond. If you want to be an inclusive leader, friend or colleague, learning how to listen without interrupting someone, finishing their sentence or wanting to justify, defend or offer a solution is important.

- Don't get defensive and don't dismiss the other person's concerns. Show empathy and be willing to engage in an open conversation. Remember to decentre yourself.

- Acknowledge that you recognise that what you said or did has had a negative impact.

- Apologise without over-apologising. Don't muddle your apology with the fact that you believe you are a good person, or that your actions were well-intentioned.

- Ask questions to understand more. Remember the power of questions. Ask open-ended questions like: 'Can you tell me more about . . . '

- Respond in a way that shows that you are willing to reflect and take their feedback into account to be more inclusive in the future. To diffuse tension and manage the impact such a conversation can have on our personal ego, have a catchphrase handy. My favourite that I use when my biases are pointed out is, 'Good catch, thanks for pointing this out. I will try to do better.' Find your own in your own communication style.

- Take time to introspect honestly and deeply. Being curious is helpful here. It may not be clear to you why what you said or did caused harm, so make the effort to educate yourself to unlearn what you thought was acceptable and learn to be more inclusive. Through curiosity, we expand our understanding about the bias and discrimination around us, which enables us to start seeing the moments when our biases are pointed out as an opportunity for growth and self-development.

Reject binary thinking

'One thing that comes up for me is that people recognise that they benefit from a system that is inherently oppressive to others. Deep down, they know. But they also don't want to address it, because it makes them feel like they're bad people.'

DEI expert

We live in an increasingly polarised world where we are conditioned by those who are in positions of power and the media to engage in dichotomous thinking. This false dichotomy, also known as false dilemma or false binary, is an informal fallacy where we falsely frame an issue as having only two options, even though more possibilities exist. If we are committed to DEI, we must be anti-white, anti-cisgender, anti-heterosexual, anti-able bodied and so on. If we identify as feminists, we must be anti-men. We assume that DEI efforts to address racism are actually an act of reverse racism without understanding that there is no such thing as reverse racism; DEI efforts aim to level the playing field and correct historical inequities. On the other hand, if we are anti-DEI, it is assumed that we are racist, sexist, homophobic, ableist, etc. Either way, taking a stand can feel severe and can come with extreme labels.

In the context of DEI, it comes back to the misinterpreted view that giving a slice of equity to one marginalised group means taking away from another group.

This is further reinforced by political discourse that pushes a combative 'good vs bad' narrative to DEI. On 30 April 2024, former US President Donald Trump told *Time* in an interview, 'I think there is a definite anti-white feeling in this country. I don't think it would be a very tough thing to address, frankly. But I think the laws are very unfair right now.'[211]

Dichotomous thinking shuts down conversations with greater nuance, and closes the space to engage our reservations and concerns, excitement and opportunities. What we need instead is to create sufficient space for multiple realities and opposite things to coexist at the same time. Being pro-DEI does not make us anti-white or anti-men. We need to be able to differentiate between systems and people. Constructively critiquing the patriarchy does not mean hatred of men. Interrogating the system of racism that devalues the life of people of colour, does not mean the hatred of white people. What we are doing instead is constructively critiquing systems of oppression and identifying who benefits from those systems and, most importantly, what needs to change to make these systems fair.

Move from debate to discussion and dialogue

To create this space for multiple realities to coexist, we need to move away from debate to discussion and dialogue. In a debate, each party has to take a stand – for or against the motion and there is only one winner. When we are engaging in a difference of opinion, we try to convince the other person of the rightness of our position. This only increases our defensiveness, as well as that of the other person, and leaves little room for increasing understanding and shifting mindset. In debating, we become more attached to our own view, rather than being open to other's views – we want to avoid 'losing' the argument. It is a form of non-relational communication where we are not using the opportunity to learn from and build our relationships with others who may hold differing views from us.

Social justice issues are not clear-cut. There are many viewpoints in the space between the extremes. We need to be able to hold space for more nuanced discussions so that we hear different perspectives, and have richer dialogues. This is what helps to shift our mindsets from being fixed to being open to growth. When we engage in discussions and dialogues rather than debates, we are open to learning about multiple perspectives while examining our own assumptions and pre-held beliefs. We can reflect on the limitations of our views while being open to consider other perspectives. So, the next time you find yourself discussing bias, discrimination or other DEI topics, resist the temptation to debate and focus on having a discussion and dialogue. You may walk away feeling enriched and open to shifting your own position on DEI-related issues.

Expand your circle

To get comfortable with multiple perspectives and life experiences, reflect on the people in your current close circle and make an effort to expand your circle to include people with varied backgrounds and life experiences.

 # Who is in your closest circle?

Step 1: Think of the people you trust the most (not including your family members).

These people are the ones you rely on. They are people you go to for advice, especially on crucial decisions. They are the people whose abilities you are confident of. They can be from your workplace, childhood, clubs, spiritual affiliations or leisure activities (even online communities). In the following table, write down the names of these people. Then, starting with the gender column, place an X for every one that defines themselves as the same gender as you. Continue with the rest of the columns. If the person does not share the same characteristic as you, leave the column blank.

Step 2: Reflect on the following questions.

Write down your reflections in your notebook.
- What did you notice about the common characteristics between yourself and your trusted 10?
- Do you tend to trust people who share your cultural background or life experiences more readily?
- Whose perspectives might you be missing? ➤

Can I say that?

Name	Gender	Sexual as orientation	Age	Physical abilities/ appearance (Do they look like me in terms of skin colour/ hair texture/ height/ weight, etc.?)	Educational background/ experiences (Have they worked in the same industry/ companies as I have?)	Personality profile	Neuroddi-vergence	Nationality/ ethnicity/ cultural background/ religious	Marital status and/or parenthood choices	Socio-economic background

Checklist

In your journey in letting go of the fear of discomfort through vulnerability, have you:
- ☐ taken the time to recognise and acknowledge the discomfort that you may be experiencing?
- ☐ resisted the temptation to play discrimination Olympics?
- ☐ made an effort to centre the discomfort of others?
- ☐ sought out personal narratives of people different from yourself?
- ☐ paused before reacting to seek out alternative perspectives or reflect on why you are feeling triggered?
- ☐ adjusted the ways in which you respond when your own biases are pointed out?
- ☐ engaged in more discussions and dialogues, rather than debates?
- ☐ expanded your circle of people you trust?

 # Stop-Start-Continue

To become more vulnerable and let go of the fear of discomfort, write down in your notebook what you are going to stop doing, start doing and continue doing from now on based on the tools in this chapter.

To let go of our fear of discomfort, we need to be vulnerable. This vulnerability enables us to turn the perceived threats of DEI to opportunities, and we can do this by getting comfortable with the discomfort, engaging for progress to advance DEI efforts and by engaging in greater discussion and dialogue.

Chapter 7

Let go of the fear of taking action and its personal consequences with courage

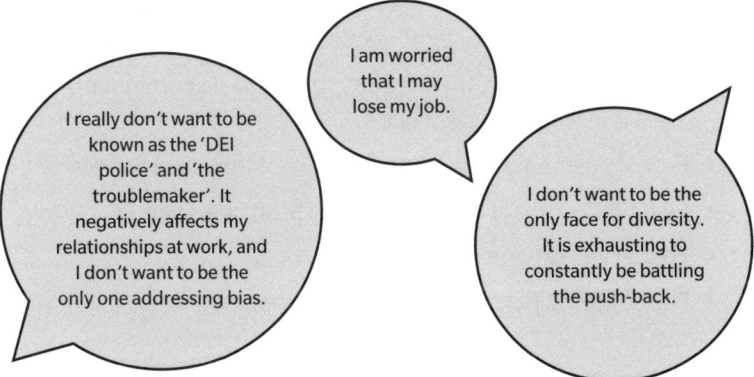

I am worried that I may lose my job.

I really don't want to be known as the 'DEI police' and 'the troublemaker'. It negatively affects my relationships at work, and I don't want to be the only one addressing bias.

I don't want to be the only face for diversity. It is exhausting to constantly be battling the push-back.

The fear of taking DEI-related action and its personal consequences

Those of us who work with DEI initiatives – as DEI leaders and practitioners, HR/talent management professionals, business leaders and colleagues – are often fearful of the consequences of supporting DEI-related actions. This fear shows up in many different ways. We may be worried about how being seen as the 'DEI-police' will impact our relationships with colleagues. We may worry that we won't get the support and resourcing needed to push DEI initiatives forward. We may be anxious that, given the backlash and resistance, our careers or image may be jeopardised. In extreme cases, our safety may be compromised. Many are anxious about the toll that DEI work takes on our mental and physical well-being. The pressure to be 'perfect' and always say the right thing so that one's competence or professionalism is not questioned can be a real source of worry. For those from marginalised groups in leadership positions, there is the added expectation of holding the flag for all underrepresented identities. This added pressure can be overwhelming and cause anxiety.

Fear of taking DEI-related actions and its personal consequences encapsulates the following accompanying fears:

- Fear of losing friendships and relationships.
- Fear of being in situations of conflict or confrontation with colleagues when one addresses inequity, bias and discrimination that are witnessed or experienced.
- Fear of addressing the inequity, bias and discrimination that are witnessed or experienced.
- Fear of push-back or lack of commitment from decision makers.
- Fear of the impact of addressing bias on one's career.
- Fear of DEI fatigue or burnout.
- Fear of being perceived as the token hire.

- Fear of the impact of addressing bias on how one is perceived by others.
- Fear of the impact of being seen as the 'DEI/woke police'.
- Fear for one's personal safety.
- Fear of losing one's livelihood.

Do you recognise any of these fears in yourself?

Once we have become aware of this fear, the question is – how do we let go of it? The answer involves addressing the root cause of the fear of taking DEI-related actions and its personal consequences – the negative outcomes that can occur. We know that we need to act. We need to translate our intention into action. But when the action has the potential to result in negative outcomes for us, how do we keep going? To keep at it requires courage – being brave and having the strength to keep going in spite of the possible negative personal consequences while continuing to find ways to address bias and discrimination, all while protecting your mental and physical health and safety. Courage enables us to stop seeing DEI as a threat, and instead focus on the purpose of DEI, which is to nurture inclusive, diverse and equitable workplaces. The next question is, how can we develop the courage we require?

Developing courage

Develop your DEI purpose statement

'So when I go to leaders today, they would all say, "Yes, yes, we should do it [DEI initiatives]." But at the end of day no one is doing anything. But it's the right thing to say, because they're afraid to say the wrong thing in this field.'

HR leader

What is your *why*?

Why are you involved in DEI initiatives? Why does it matter to you?

In the tough moments, when we encounter fears or experience back-lash and push-back from colleagues and leaders, it is our personal *why* that acts as our anchor, keeping us grounded. Our why gives us the courage we require to continue the work.

Even if you have a good idea of your purpose for engaging in DEI activities, it can be helpful to review it and obtain even greater clarity. In the book, *Leading through Bias*, the authors write:[212]

> *'Leading through bias requires you to believe wholeheartedly in the purpose of Diversity, Equity and Inclusion (DEI). It requires you to lead with conviction. Leading with conviction is not about political correctness, trying to be "woke" or "keeping up" with the latest business trends that everyone else is following.*
>
> *Leading with conviction means being convinced that (1) inequity and inequality exist, and that they need to be addressed, (2) being more inclusive and equitable is the right thing to do, and finally, (3) your organisation will be better because of it. Do you have that conviction?'*

 ## My DEI purpose statement

Through the following steps, you will create a DEI purpose statement for yourself. This statement will be your anchor, providing you with the courage to let go of the fears that often arise from engaging in DEI efforts.

Step 1: Identify the values that are important to you when engaging in DEI efforts.

Below is a list of some value words that may help you in making your list. Circle as many as possible that are important to you in doing the work related to DEI. Feel free to add additional value words that may not be featured in this list.

Authenticity	Contribution	Happiness	Loyalty	Responsibility
Achievement	Creativity	Honesty	Meaningful work	Security
Authority	Curiosity	Humour	Openness	Self-respect
Autonomy	Determination	Influence	Optimism	Service
Balance	Fairness	Justice	Peace	Stability
Boldness	Faith	Kindness	Pleasure	Success
Compassion	Fame	Knowledge	Popularity	Status
Challenge	Friendships	Leadership	Recognition	Trustworthiness
Community	Fun	Learning	Reputation	Wealth
Competency	Growth	Love	Respect	Wisdom

From the words that you have circled, pick the top three values that are most important to you as you engage in DEI efforts. Write them down in your notebook.

Step 2: Reflect on what you hope the DEI efforts that you engage in will achieve.

You may think about it in the following ways:[213]

- *Representation:* to increase representation of the number and the voice of members of underrepresented groups.
- *Participation:* to create opportunities for meaningful and active participation in DEI activities.
- *Appreciation:* to recognise the benefits of DEI for all employees.
- *Application:* to see efforts being made to embed DEI principles into organisational structures, systems, practices, policies and culture.

Pick out two to three short phrases that reflect what you hope your efforts will achieve. Write them down in your notebook. ➤

Step 3: Put together your DEI purpose statement.
Complete the below statement: I engage in DEI efforts to [fill in the two to three words or phrases from Step 2] with [insert the three values from Step 1].

You are welcome to reword the above sentence to make it your own. Let this statement be your anchor to provide you with the courage to do this work. Print it out and place it somewhere to remind you of why you do the DEI work you do.

Know what to expect

'There is also the fear that it will not be received well. They were hoping that I would make it gentler for the ears to listen; to change hearts and minds.'

DEI expert

What if I lose my job?

What if my colleagues view me as the 'DEI or woke police' and avoid engaging with me? I won't have any friends at work.

What if someone verbally or physically attacks me at work for being pro-DEI?

Are these familiar to you?

It is natural to have negative thoughts and think about what can go wrong. But, sometimes, this can spin out of control and distort reality. Imagining even a modest amount of disappointment, failure or embarrassment can be a cause of fear or despair – a catastrophe. This is what psychologists would refer to as catastrophising or assuming that the worst-case scenario is the likely outcome, or thinking that a situation is worse than it really is. This fear of the negative personal consequences of engaging in DEI efforts can hold us back from engaging even when we want to.

Drawing on the practice of visualisation in cognitive behavioural therapy to help reframe and modify negative thought patterns and behaviours, it can be helpful to visualise what would happen if you did or did not engage in DEI initiatives. This is not easy and requires courage to visualise the worst-case outcomes that could happen in both scenarios.

Start by first acknowledging that you may be catastrophising. Remind yourself that you have engaged in DEI efforts before, and they have turned out fine.

Next, close your eyes and visualise what the worst-case situation may look and feel like. Think about the worst things that could happen if you chose to engage in a DEI effort such as addressing someone's bias or act of discrimination. Visualise the people involved and what they may say or do. Visualise how you may react. Visualise what you might say or do, or perhaps not say or do. Think about how you may feel. Continue to keep your eyes closed and visualise what would happen if you chose not to engage in the same DEI effort of addressing someone's bias or act of discrimination. How would you feel? How would the various people involved feel? What might the people involved say or do? What could the consequences be?

Open your eyes, take a deep breath (or two) and reflect on the following:

- Remind yourself of your DEI purpose statement. Take a moment to ground yourself in why you are involved in DEI efforts in the first place.

- Ask yourself: is the worst-case scenario that you imagined in the visualisation exercise likely to happen? If you said yes, how likely is it to happen? Think about what conditions are necessary for the worst-case scenario to occur.

- Think about all the times when your engagement with DEI has gone well, and when you have had positive interactions with your colleagues.

- Think about all the times when your engagement with DEI has not gone well, and reflect on what you could have done differently to prevent the negative outcomes.

- Take a moment to remind yourself of the benefits of DEI, and what it does for people of underrepresented and marginalised groups.

- Think about what the consequences might be if you did not engage in DEI efforts and allowed the bias or discrimination to continue to exist for the people involved. Reflect on how that would make you feel.

- Reflect on how you could engage in DEI efforts to prevent your worst-case scenario from occurring. What could you do differently from what you have done before? Could you change the way you approach the situation? Could you use a different tone or language when speaking about the issues at hand? Could you seek support from a colleague when addressing the issue?

Plan your move

'So at a really baseline level, I fear offending people more often than not. On a daily basis, I have friends who just say things in conversation. You're in the height of fun. You're laughing. You're having a glass of wine, and then they say something. I'm now more alert and aware to it, and sensitive to it but you don't want to disrupt the flow of a girl's night out. You want to be cool. There have been so many moments when I've said nothing, and then, of course, I beat myself up after, because I'm like, how are you a feminist when you allow that to slide. So I fear offending people, and most of all my friends all the time.'

Business leader

One of the most challenging DEI actions is addressing bias and discrimination. It is difficult to be in situations of conflict or friction with colleagues when addressing the inequity, bias and discrimination that are witnessed or experienced. We may fear how we will be perceived by others for addressing bias, and fear the impact it has on our career. To let go of these fears requires us to engage in courageous conversations. In courageous conversations, individuals are encouraged to share their views openly and honestly, avoiding defensiveness or blame. A crucial element of these discussions is a willingness to learn by embracing the friction – and the discomfort that comes from it – as an opportunity to learn. Such conversations require us to be, and stay, engaged even through the discomfort while speaking our truth, all while understanding that immediate resolution might not be achievable, and patience may be necessary. Think of this discomfort as useful friction that helps us to let go of our fear and make progress happen. Turns out that discomfort, and conflict, are essential to 'genius teams', teams that can handle more complexity than their peers. According to psychologist and author Merete Wedell-Wedellsborg, 'discomforting moments motivate them [genius teams] and inspire new ideas'.[214]

How can we have these courageous conversations?

When you witness or experience a bias or act of discrimination, you have a few options: you can choose not to address it, address it at the time when it occurred, or address it at a later time. These three choices are always available to you. There may be situations in which it may be unsafe to address the bias or discrimination that you have witnessed or experienced, and you may choose not to do so. In the case of obvious acts of discrimination such as sexual harassment, racism, homophobia, etc., refer to your organisation's policy on reporting these incidents. Many organisations have a whistle-blower policy to protect employees who raise such harmful acts of discrimination. Hopefully, those situations are infrequent. Most biases and acts of discrimination can and should be addressed; as an ally committed to DEI, allowing biases to exist should not be an option.

Courageous conversations come into the picture when we are speaking of non-extreme acts. This might be someone cracking an inappropriate joke at lunch, interrupting someone during a meeting, stealing an idea and claiming it as their own, or even a casual comment or compliment that reflects a negative stereotype.

In these situations, it is important to address the bias and act of discrimination. And yet, when we are confronted with bias – either experiencing it ourselves or witnessing it – we are often at a loss for words, even if we are trained for this. We might muster up an uncomfortable laugh, expression or response, hoping that the discomfort in the room will go away. We may quickly change the topic of conversation to ease the discomfort. We might not address the bias because we don't have the right tools to do so and fear the walls of defence that are likely to come up. Knowing what to say and how to say it are crucial to navigating these situations. Planning these conversations ahead of time can be extremely helpful to reduce the stress of the situation. That way, we can get comfortable with the discomfort and sit with it through these courageous conversations.

Here are some tips for planning your move.

Despite the fear of the personal consequences of doing so, if you choose to address the bias and discrimination, keep the following in mind when engaging in a courageous conversation.

The power of questions

No one likes to be confronted about their bias, and the human reaction to confrontation is to become defensive. Given this, biases need to be addressed in a non-confrontational way – our tone matters. Asking questions in the right tone can be a powerful tool for getting those around us to have an 'aha' moment, one in which they discover a bias they weren't aware of. If you witness a discriminatory view being expressed at lunch, you could ask the person this: that's an interesting way of looking at it, why don't you tell me more? It may open up for a rich discussion at lunch where all parties learn from each other's viewpoints.

Engage in an empathetic dialogue

One of the best ways to prevent the walls of defence from going up is to approach these conversations to address bias and discrimination with empathy. Remember that today it is someone else's bias that we are pointing out. Tomorrow, it could very well be our own. After all, we are all biased. Engaging in an empathetic dialogue in the spirit of helping the other person grow and develop is key.

Are you ready to plan your move?

Planning your move

With the steps laid out in this chapter, hopefully you feel better equipped to address biases. Planning your move can be helpful and this exercise will help you do just that. The first few times will be hard but the more comfortable we get at using questions and comments to engage courageously on biases, the easier it becomes.

Imagine a bias that has been said or done to you or that you have witnessed being said or done to someone else. How would you respond? You can use the guide below to help you along.

Describe the bias. Can you name the bias?

Have you:

☐ experienced it yourself?
☐ witnessed it happening to someone else?

Would you address the bias:

☐ at the time it occurred?
☐ at a later time?

If you are addressing the bias at the time it was communicated, which question(s)/comment(s) would you use?

☐ I didn't understand the joke, would you be able to please explain it to me?
☐ Why don't you tell me more about your choice of words here?
☐ Why do you think that?
☐ What was your intention in saying that? Do you think your intention may have been different from the impact of your words?
☐ I'm curious. What did you mean by that?
☐ That's an interesting way of looking at it, why don't you tell me more?
☐ Can you help me understand why you reacted that way?
☐ Hang on, I don't believe _____ had finished sharing their thoughts.

➤

- ☐ Thank you for paraphrasing _____ idea, that is indeed very refreshing.
- ☐ Hang on, I'm sure _____ understands this well and does not need an explanation.
- ☐ How did you get to that decision/conclusion?
- ☐ What led you to draw that conclusion?
- ☐ How do you know it is working? What evidence would you have to demonstrate that?
- ☐ Have you looked at other options? What were they and why was this the best way forward?

If you are addressing the bias at a later time, don't wait too long. You don't want to be in a situation where the relevant parties have forgotten the context in which the bias happened. Involve HR, depending on the severity of the situation, or if you need support. This may be especially helpful when there is a power imbalance between yourself and the other person, like when the person who is being biased is your manager or your CEO. Planning out what you may say is very helpful. You can of course choose your own sentences that reflect your own style of communication. The suggestions here are only to guide you along the journey.

Step 1: Invite the person who engaged in the bias to a meeting. How would you start the conversation?
'I would like to speak to you about something on my mind. I understand that this can be uncomfortable, but I would appreciate it if you let me finish what I have to say before we discuss it.'

Step 2: Explain clearly what was said or done. Details always help so the person can't deny it.
'In the meeting the other day, you said/did . . . '

Step 3: Explain how it made you/someone else feel. Allow enough room in your explanation to give the person space to respond later.

'When you said/did _____, it seems like you are _____, but I am not sure if this is what you mean. However, what you said/did made me/the other person feel . . . I would like you to imagine how it must have felt for me/the other person.'

Imagine that the person gets defensive, how would you respond?
'I understand that you may have said/done this unintentionally, but I would really like you to let me finish.'

'I understand this is hard for you, but please do not dismiss this life experience of mine/theirs. It has had an impact and I would like to engage in a constructive dialogue about this once I finish sharing my side. After all, we all have biases, right?'

Step 4: Offer suggestions for what the person can do differently. Use credible data or research to support why you have brought this up.
'Research/data shows us that . . . In the future, it would be better if you . . . '

Step 5: Give the other person time to reflect and respond.

'I know this is a lot to process. Would you like to take a moment and then we can discuss this? I would like us to find a way forward.'

- -

Prioritise self-care

> *'I also think about the possibility of burning out. I could burn out of this. On hard days with bad experiences, I fantasise about just packing it all up and just focusing in on my other work.'*
>
> **DEI expert**

Being engaged in DEI initiatives and addressing bias and discrimination is not easy. In fact, it is often challenging, especially understanding that it takes time to achieve positive change towards inclusive, equitable and diverse workplaces. While some may have DEI embedded into their job descriptions, there are many others who do this work voluntarily, finding time and energy to plan and execute DEI initiatives in their organisations beyond their job scope. This kind of work is known as *kinkeeping*[215] which is used to describe the invisible work that often goes without credit, and encapsulates the physical and emotional unpaid labour that accompanies DEI efforts.

This means that those engaged with DEI initiatives have to have the courage to say that they need support, draw boundaries to protect their mental and emotional health and to even take a break occasionally to come back stronger. This is not easy to do. For those of us who work in the DEI space, who feel passionately about its goals, some may see these acts as a sign of weakness. Some of us may even see it as 'giving in' to the backlash and resistance. It requires courage to recognise that to preserve in the long run requires us to prioritise self-care.

According to Mary-Frances Winters, author of the book, *Black Fatigue: How Racism Erodes the Mind, Body and Spirit*, the emotional toll of DEI work is 'the extra effort it takes daily to be personally subjected to microaggressions, discrimination, inequities, and/or violence, or hear the stories of such from others and be able to manage the fear, frustration, anger and other emotions that result'.[216] Many of us who work to implement DEI initiatives do so because we have gone through personal experiences of bias and discrimination and don't want others to endure the same. However, when those working with DEI are the targets of the backlash, they are subject to re-harm.

In recent years, there has been a growing focus on the emotional, mental and physical toll of working with DEI. Given this, what should you be looking out for?

- *Diversity fatigue, burnout and weathering.*
  Diversity fatigue is a term that was first used in the 1990s in the USA and is used to describe the tiredness from an endless effort in DEI without seeing enough progress. While some researchers focus on understanding 'majority groups' feelings of weariness toward diversity efforts'[217] diversity fatigue is something we see among DEI professionals working with DEI, regardless of whether they belong to the well-represented or underrepresented groups. This fatigue

occurs from the disappointment of the slow pace of progress or the lack of support from the top management.

Diversity fatigue occurs because companies and leaders may feel that there is no value to be gained from DEI which, in turn, results in a lack of enthusiasm and commitment, reduced resourcing and minimum efforts. Among DEI leaders and participants alike, the burnout as a result of this fatigue is quite apparent and is characterised by the backlash and resistance that we have looked at earlier in this book. This burnout is further amplified in parts of the world where DEI professionals are also wearing other hats. About 60% of chief diversity officers (CDOs) in Asia Pacific wear a double hat, with responsibility for DEI, HR, talent and CSR. That's 18 percentage points more than in EMEA and 21 percentage points more than in the USA.

The stress experienced by DEI professionals and those from marginalised groups is cumulative and 'repeated exposure to socioeconomic adversity, political marginalization, racism, and perpetual discrimination can harm health'.[218] This is known as weathering. In a 2006 article,[219] researchers linked biomarkers like cortisol levels, sympathetic nerve activity, blood pressure reactivity, cytokine production, waist-to-hip ratio and glycated haemoglobin level to social measures, including socioeconomic status, occupation, birth outcome and environmental risk. In doing so, they measured the 'allostatic load' which refers to the physiological 'cost' of chronic, or repeated, exposure to stress. What they found was that black adults had higher allostatic load scores than white adults, and had a greater probability of a high score at all ages, particularly at 35–64 years.

- *Loneliness and isolation.*
  DEI professionals often experience intense loneliness and isolation. Some may feel they are carrying the weight of marginalised communities on their shoulders. If they belong to a marginalised community themselves, it might make the isolation and loneliness worse. If backlash and resistance forces them to repeatedly

convince their leaders of the importance of their work, it can lead to even further isolation.

- *Emotional triggers during DEI workshops and discussions.*
  Catastrophising has been linked to a number of adverse experiences and behaviours, including anxiety, depression and anger-related problems. The topic of DEI causes discomfort. We are asking ourselves and others to reflect on our bias, and on how our bias negatively impacts others. The conversations that happen during DEI workshops and discussions can be uncomfortable and stressful for both DEI professionals and participants/colleagues. In fact, one could say that the success of DEI initiatives hinges on getting comfortable with the discomfort. During the DEI workshops that I run for leaders, I often start by saying that they should expect to get uncomfortable and, if they don't get uncomfortable at some point during the workshop, I will give them their money back.

To manage these emotions, DEI professionals sometimes end up engaging in surface acting, where they try to fabricate positive emotions when they do not feel positive and suppress the negative emotions they do feel.[220] These reactions are further exacerbated by display rules – implicit or explicit rules that dictate appropriate expression and suppression of emotions in the workplace.[221] These rules are not written or well-understood. Instead, they are subtle and assumed, meaning that DEI professionals are expected to keep calm and carry on.

- *Short tenures and limited career development opportunities.*
  Research on the experiences of DEI professionals and HR professionals doing significant DEI work in their roles found that, despite their roles being high-status, well-compensated jobs, they endured extensive burnout and high turnover.[222] In fact, the average tenure of people in these roles is just three years. In addition, we know that DEI leaders find it challenging to transition to other executive roles in the organisation, such as CMO, CTO, CPO and COO.[223] This suggests that the role is often perceived as unique and not considered to be a qualification for other executive positions.

All of these are further reasons why it is important to prioritise your self-care. DEI will not be 'solved' by 2025 or 2050. There is no end date, we are in it for the long haul.

Find allies and support systems

I cannot stress this enough. In doing this work for many years, finding allies and a support system is crucial. Allies support you. They are people who cheer you on and support you when things don't go so well. They are people who may be from inside or outside the organisation, who will act as guideposts and advise you on how to approach difficult or sensitive topics. Alongside allies, have a core group who forms your support system. These are the people who offer a judgement-free space to vent, check on each other and who provide emotional support when needed.

Process your feelings

In DEI workshops on bias awareness, those confronting their biases may feel defensiveness, doubt, guilt, shame and/or denial. On the other hand, those on the receiving end of the bias may feel resentment, pain, anger, helplessness and/or sadness. There are DEI professionals who work with DEI who sit at the intersection of both these groups who may feel both.

Individuals involved in DEI work should first focus on their mental health by identifying the burnout signs and taking active measures to tackle them. Processing one's emotions is a crucial measure in self-care. You can process your feelings yourself or with someone in your support system. It begins with asking 'What am I feeling?' and 'Why am I feeling this?' and getting specific. This requires you to show yourself grace and space to get vulnerable in acknowledging your emotions, giving yourself permission to be uncomfortable, and encouraging yourself to have courageous conversations with yourself. This puts some distance between the physical reaction you may be feeling – like your hands shaking because you're feeling threatened during a discussion – and the reason behind that reaction, allowing you to fully unpack what is going on.

Set boundaries

For those of us working with DEI, there is often a real passion and inner desire to make our workplaces inclusive, diverse and equitable. At the same time, given how taxing this work is, it is important to set boundaries. These boundaries will look different for different people. It requires us to figure out what aspect of DEI work is most emotionally draining to us, and not doing that work.

For someone, it could be engaging in DEI as long as there is no hint of a personal safety threat or risk to their livelihood. For others, there may be a red line that should not be crossed to protect their self-image and reputation. For some who are DEI professionals and also from a marginalised group, the boundary could be not speaking on behalf of an entire group, for example a black employee speaking about black experiences. It is essential to develop awareness about the right time to retreat and recharge, which will facilitate consistent involvement in DEI initiatives for the long haul.

Show yourself grace and compassion

Remember that transforming our organisation's systems and culture to be inclusive and equitable is going to take time. There is no easy fix. This means that it is important to manage your expectations of yourself and of others. Set realistic expectations about what DEI initiatives can accomplish in the short term while always having the long-term goals in sight. This is a good mechanism to control frustration and keep motivation at the required level, even when the progress seems slow. And along the way, be sure to celebrate progress, no matter how small. Identifying and celebrating small milestones can provide motivation and affirm the importance of continuous DEI efforts.

Checklist

In your journey in letting go of the fear of taking action and its personal consequences through courage, have you:

☐ developed your DEI purpose statement?

☐ taken the time to visualise and reflect on possible scenarios of engaging with DEI initiatives?

☐ made a plan for what to do when you witness or experience bias and discrimination?

☐ leveraged the power of questions to engage in an empathetic dialogue about bias and discrimination?

☐ found allies and support systems?

☐ taken time to process your feelings?

☐ set boundaries?

☐ shown yourself grace and compassion?

Stop-Start-Continue

To become more courageous and let go of the fear of taking DEI-related actions and its personal consequences, write down in your notebook what you are going to stop doing, start doing and continue doing from now on based on the tools in this chapter.

To let go of our fear of taking DEI-related actions and our fear of the personal consequences of doing so, we need to be courageous. This courage enables us to turn the perceived threats of DEI to opportunities, and we can do this by anchoring ourselves in our DEI purpose statement, visualising the worst-case scenario to know what to expect, planning our move to address bias and dist

Chapter 8

Let go of the fear of a lack of positive impact with resilience

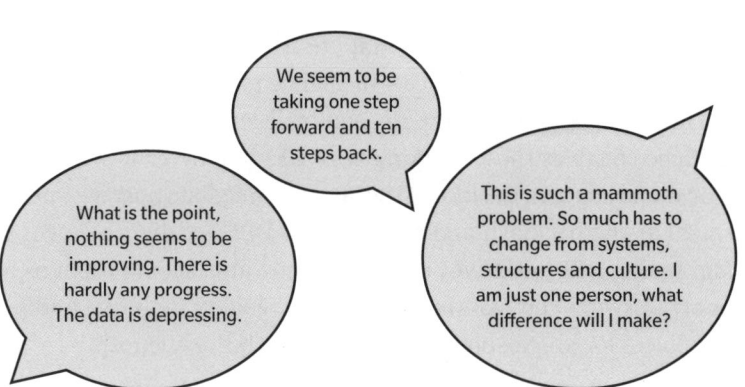

Fear of the lack of positive impact

Have you ever felt helpless – that no matter what you say or do, it won't change things and make your workplace inclusive, so what is the point of doing anything? Those of us who work with DEI initiatives – as DEI leaders and practitioners, HR/talent management professionals, business leaders and colleagues – have all likely felt this at some point in time or the other.

Fear of the lack of positive impact encapsulates the following accompanying fears:

- Fear of the negative impact of performative DEI work.
- Fear of not having a significant enough impact.

Do you recognise any of these fears in yourself?

Once we have become aware of this fear, the question is – how do we let go of it? The answer involves addressing the root cause of the fear of the lack of positive impact – underestimating how long it actually takes to nurture organisations that are truly diverse, equitable and inclusive. It requires resilience – resilience to persevere for the long haul towards the goal of a diverse, equitable and inclusive workplace. Resilience enables those working with DEI initiatives to withstand, recover and adapt in the face of the lack of immediate positive impact, as well as the backlash and resistance to DEI. Resilience moves us from seeing DEI initiatives as a threat, towards seeing them as an opportunity to keep working towards the goal of inclusive and fair workplaces for all. So, how can we develop this resilience?

Developing Resilience

Be patient

'I just worry that this could all be for nothing if the systems aren't really being changed. That we're just effectively creating a more diverse teaching force. But in doing that, we're throwing teachers of colour into a burning house. Right? If the education system is not being fixed, what the hell is the point of diversifying it? Because you're just traumatising more folks of colour.'

DEI expert

In our fast-paced existence of today, we expect that our actions will yield results – the outcomes we want – quickly. In our organisations, we reward people who are able to achieve outcomes quickly. We set KPIs and OKRs with tight deadlines and evaluate progress against these.

When it comes to our organisation's DEI initiatives, we need to rethink that approach. The lack of diverse representation, inequitable systems and structures and non-inclusive cultures stems from a systemic and institutional bias that has deep roots in colonisation, slavery and a capitalist approach. The combination of colonialism and capitalism emphasised class differentiation alongside gender and race, and regarded white men as the superior class of societies.[224] Dismantling these systems of oppression, power structures and the resulting culture and social conditioning will take time.

There is *no* easy fix. We need to be in this for the long haul.

Systemic and cultural bias have been built over centuries and will take time to dismantle and replace with inclusive systems, structures and cultures. These oppressive systems and cultures are deeply embedded into the fabric of our daily life. As we have seen in examples throughout this book, human beings resist change. We need to have patience. In this regard, patience does not mean we should not act to dismantle non-inclusive structures and cultures, but we must also have realistic expectations of the speed at which we will see impact.

Start small and build

I am a realistic optimist. I believe that the change that is needed happens through frequent and consistent day-to-day actions. Yes, we need the occasional grand gesture like public commitments and pledges or sponsorship of Pride parades and Black History month events or high-level DEI Councils, but what we really need are frequent and consistent actions by as many people as possible. Think of these smaller actions as building the foundation we need to construct a new and inclusive structure. It takes time but, once in place, the building goes up quickly. With a strong foundation in place, we can move faster, building diverse, equitable and inclusive workplaces. At the same time, remember to watch for burnout and prioritise self-care along the way.

We have seen how harmful microaggressions or 'termite biases' are. To counter these small and subtle but very harmful non-inclusive behaviours, we need microaffirmations, microvalidations and microinclusions. These are the small, subtle and impactful behaviours in which we can nurture greater inclusion and equity with colleagues and among team members.

According to Adjunct Professor Mary Rowe at the MIT Sloan School of Management, microaffirmations are 'apparently small acts, which are often ephemeral and hard-to-see, events that are public and private, often unconscious but very effective, which occur wherever people wish to help others to succeed'.[225] Microaffirmations and microinclusions are signals that indicate value and respect to build inclusivity.[226] In their *Harvard Business Review* article, 'An Antidote to Microaggressions? Microvalidations', Laura Morgan Roberts, Megan Grayson and Brook Dennard Rosser define microvalidations as 'small, positive actions that encourage or affirm'.[227]

What are examples of microaffirmations, microvalidations or microinclusions?[228]

- *Acknowledge presence.*
  Smile, nod and make eye contact when someone speaks. Don't interrupt and disrupt interruptions. Avoid ghosting – abruptly ending communication without explanation – people from marginalised groups.

- *Validate identity.*
  Respect people's intersectional identity. Use their names and pronouns as they wish to be known. When in doubt ask: 'Am I saying your name correctly?' and don't be afraid to say: 'I haven't come across your name before, could I please check how you pronounce it?' In addition, don't assume things about someone's identity. For example, that a man's partner is a woman. When in doubt, always seek clarification.

- *Appreciate everyone's contribution.*
  Value people's contributions and input. Don't take credit for someone else's contributions and redirect stolen credit.

- *Hold people to high standards.*
  Check your low expectations of people from marginalised groups and challenge your assumptions that someone from a marginalised group will not be able to handle a challenging task. Give career advancing and actionable feedback to everyone.

- *Affirm leadership potential.*
  Recognise leadership potential in people from marginalised groups and sponsor them actively by amplifying their voice and inviting them into spaces they don't have access to, boosting them to be considered for opportunities, connecting them with people in your network and defending them when their competency is challenged.[229]

As you consider what you are going to do, remember to focus on progress and not perfection. As we have seen throughout this book, we are likely to make mistakes. Use them to unlearn, learn and grow in our inclusive mindset. Focus on your actions and ensure they are inclusive, and let go of attachment to the outcome or results. The results will come; it just may not be at the time or in the way that you expect. Keeping focused on the actions helps channel our energy towards what is needed, rather than dissipating energy worrying about the outcome.

Small actions have a ripple effect. Just like when we drop a pebble into a still lake and watch the ripples spread, I believe that every inclusive action can create positive ripples and encourage others to be inclusive as well.

Make systemic and cultural change happen

In reflecting on the progress DEI has made (or not made), I am reminded of the work of one of the most influential researchers in business management, US psychologist, Frederick Irving Herzberg. Herzberg's two-factor theory argues that job satisfaction is influenced by two different factors known as hygiene factors and motivator factors. Hygiene factors prevent employees from being dissatisfied but don't do anything to promote satisfaction. What makes employees satisfied are what are known as motivator factors.

If we apply this to DEI, performative DEI efforts are hygiene factors. Organisations – and their leaders – do the bare minimum, driven largely by legislative compliance and/or to pacify internal grassroots concerns, merely keeping their employees from dissatisfaction. It is those organisations that are truly committed, putting in genuine efforts to address systemic and cultural bias rooted in leadership support and resourcing – motivator factors – where we see that employees are satisfied. This can involve implementing inclusive hiring and talent development practices that block bias, ongoing and comprehensive DEI and cross-cultural training and creating well-resourced Employee Resource Groups (ERGs).

Beware of performative actions. Ask yourself if what you are engaging in is addressing the systemic, structural and cultural inequities and bias that exist. Every time you engage in or consider engaging in a DEI activity, ask yourself the following question: is this activity going to block bias and dismantle bias in an organisational system, structure, process or culture to make the organisation more inclusive?

Keep litmus testing your actions to ensure that what you are doing is a motivator to keep you on the right track.

Systemic DEI activities

What kind of systemic DEI activities would you like to engage in to improve inclusion in your team and organisation? While this book has focused primarily on cultural change, below is a set of questions to help us decide which systemic DEI actions are needed. Tick the ones that you would like to address.

Questions to ask yourself across the employee life cycle:

☐ Are our employees representative of society and our customers?

☐ Are our job advertisements inclusive? Have we made efforts to neutralise the language used in our job ads to attract talent from diverse backgrounds to apply?

☐ Do our job ads state that having diverse perspectives, experiences, skills and backgrounds is something the company is looking for?

☐ Have we advertised for the role as far and wide as possible?

☐ When shortlisting candidates, are we masking the CVs and other documents by removing the following identifiers – photo, name, age, gender, address, university name?

☐ Is the recruitment and selection panel representative of the diversity we would like to see in the company?

☐ Have all the members of the recruitment and selection panel been through regular bias awareness training?

☐ Are we using structured interview questions for all candidates? Is each interviewer on the panel asking the same question?

☐ Are all candidates having the same recruitment experience? Is there a standard process for all candidates? Are we putting some candidates from underrepresented groups through additional rounds of interviews or additional tasks?

☐ Can we do interviews differently from the traditional set-up to be more inclusive to neurodivergent and disabled talent? ➤

- ☐ Do we have a clear criteria-based selection process, one that includes the diversity of perspectives, experiences, skills and backgrounds that is clearly stated in the job ad? Does the candidate bring something different to the team to add value?
- ☐ Are the people hired the best-qualified candidate who met all the criteria including bringing different perspectives, experiences, skills and backgrounds? How similar is the selected person to others in the team? Does the person fit into the team or organisation's cookie cutter shape? Could you have underestimated the person? Would the person add real value to the team?
- ☐ Are some groups in our company given more career opportunities than others?
- ☐ Do we have adequate parental leave, grandparent leave, menstrual leave options that are inclusive to all?
- ☐ Do we provide feedback fairly to all employees? Do some employees get more frequent and career-advancing feedback than others?
- ☐ Are our spaces inclusive to all employees? Are the facilities in our workplace accessible and inclusive? Do we have gender-neutral toilets and menstrual products in them? Do we have a nursing room and prayer room on site? Do we have quiet spaces for employees who would prefer working there? Are our social events inclusive to different food and alcohol consumption preferences? Are our team-building events inclusive to neurodivergent individuals? Have we consulted with people from marginalised groups on what their needs are, or are we assuming what they may need?
- ☐ Do we offer hybrid, flexible working options? Are managers trained to be supportive of these?
- ☐ Have we conducted a pay equity exercise to uncover if we have unjustified pay gaps across gender identities, race or ethnic identities, functional groups, etc.? Have we made efforts to correct pay gaps identified from a pay equity exercise?
- ☐ Are our employees addressing bias and discrimination that they witness or experience in their meetings, at lunch or more generally in the organisation? Do we have mechanisms in place for employees to feel safe to address bias and discrimination?

Questions to ask yourself in the development of products and services:

☐ Are our products and services catering for a representative customer base?

☐ Are we testing our products and services with a representative group of customers to collect feedback on our products and services?

☐ How often do we involve a wide range of representative customers when collecting feedback when designing new products and services?

Questions to ask yourself across in marketing and customer service:

☐ Would diverse customers see themselves represented in our marketing material?

☐ Are our customer service agents trained in how to engage with different customers, or is our customer experience based on a dominant customer segment?

☐ How often do we involve diverse customers when collecting feedback on our marketing campaigns and customer service?

☐ How often do we involve diverse customers when collecting feedback to develop new marketing materials?

- -

Trust the purpose of DEI initiatives

'So the fear is of getting it right – to being able to make big change quickly enough to show results and doing it right without having any psychological safety to fail. There are a lot of eyes on the work we're getting paid to do. People want to know – what are the returns that are coming through? You need that early momentum to make change impact so that the ball gets bigger and bigger as it's rolling down the hill. But if it starts rolling down in different directions, then, you know, you're losing momentum. There's a lot riding on us. For future to happen, we need to do it right.'

DEI expert

What is the purpose of DEI initiatives? Distilled down to the core, DEI initiatives aim to level the playing field to nurture workplaces that are inclusive and diverse in representation. This means, among other things, ensuring that hiring and promotion processes are equitable, that employees are paid fairly and that products are designed to be inclusive to diverse customers. We must trust in the fact that DEI is the right thing to do. It is this trust that gives us hope in moments of despair when we see that progress is not happening, or not happening fast enough. The trust prevents us from engaging in groupthink or being influenced by anti-DEI rhetoric. Related to this is a belief in the goodness of humanity. Even though the voices of resistance are sometimes the loudest, I believe that the vast majority of us want to do the right thing. This trust in the purpose and in humanity is what keeps me going and, hopefully, will keep you going as well.

Trust is an essential component of resilience. Given that DEI initiatives need resilience, we need trust to enable resilience. When we have trust in those around us, we're more inclined to persevere through challenges, knowing that mutual support and confidence can lead to collective success. At the same time, we need a healthy dose of distrust to ensure that we don't become complacent and less resilient.[230] Trust, when coupled with shared values and actions, fosters resilience and enhances recovery outcomes when we experience setbacks, backlash and resistance.

Build your own personal DEI plan

Keeping the purpose of DEI and your own DEI purpose statement in mind, what are you going to do to ensure that your workplace is diverse in its representation, fair and equitable and a space where people feel included and like they belong? Throughout this book, you have been presented with a number of nudges and tools to consider in your journey to embrace DEI efforts. If you have completed the Stop-Start-Continue exercises at the end of each of the previous chapters, you should have a good idea of which tools and actions you want to focus your efforts on. The previous exercise in this chapter would have also given you some ideas to address systemic bias. What you have chosen to focus on is individual. What you have chosen is very much dependent on where you are in your DEI journey, the context in which you are in and your own personal sphere of influence.

Step 1: Make a list of all the DEI-related actions that you would like to take.

You can draw on what you wrote in the Stop-Start-Continue exercises, as well as from the tools and exercises in each chapter. These can be actions that help to nurture an inclusive culture, make your personal interactions more inclusive and/or actions that address systemic and structural bias. Use additional paper if needed.

Step 2: Place the actions you have written on the effort vs impact graph below (Figure 8.1).

Think about each action in terms of the effort needed to make it happen (this includes your own effort, effort of others, resources and

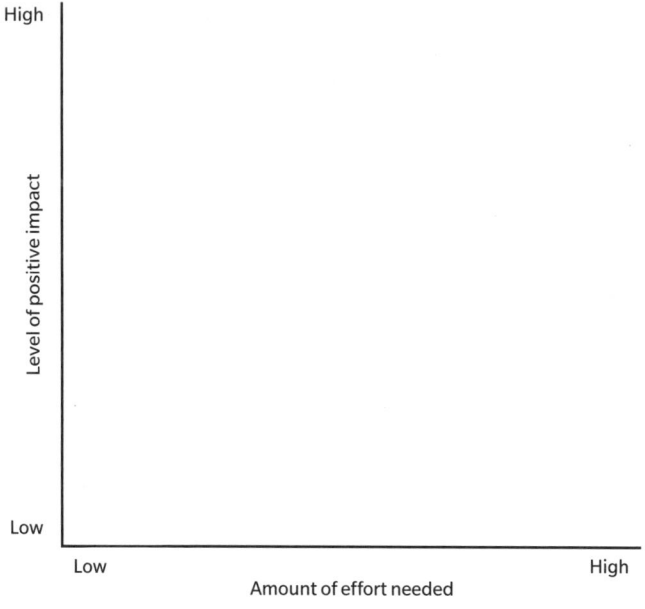

Figure 8.1 Effort vs impact graph

➤

leadership support) and the impact of the action. For each action, ask yourself how much effort is needed and what its potential impact is.

Step 3: Divide the previous graph into three vertical spaces as shown by the dotted lines below (Figure 8.2).

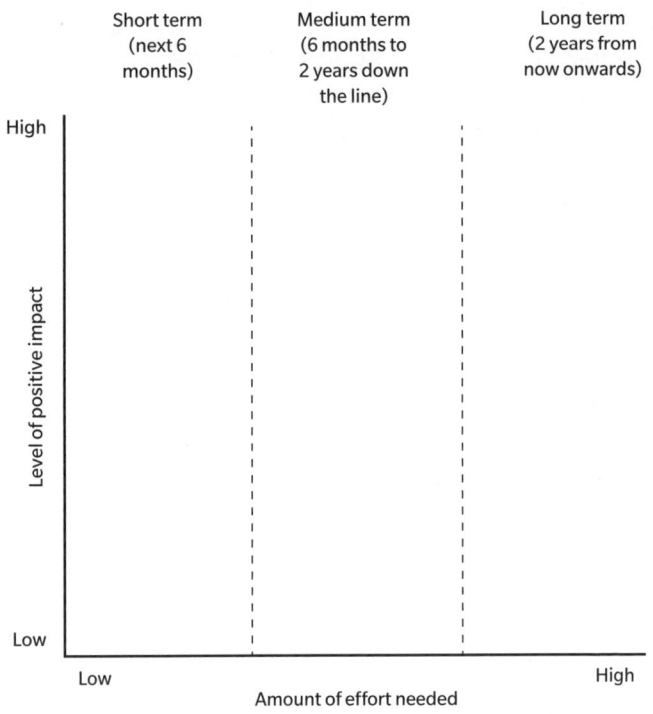

Figure 8.2 Effort vs impact graph with time frames

Each of these zones reflects the time frame in which those actions are likely to be able to be enacted.

Step 4: Focus your efforts on the actions in the shaded zone shown (Figure 8.3).

These are the actions that you should focus your energy on. These actions require low to medium effort and result in medium to high impact. The actions that need greater effort and also have significant positive impact are those that you should keep in view to engage in at a later

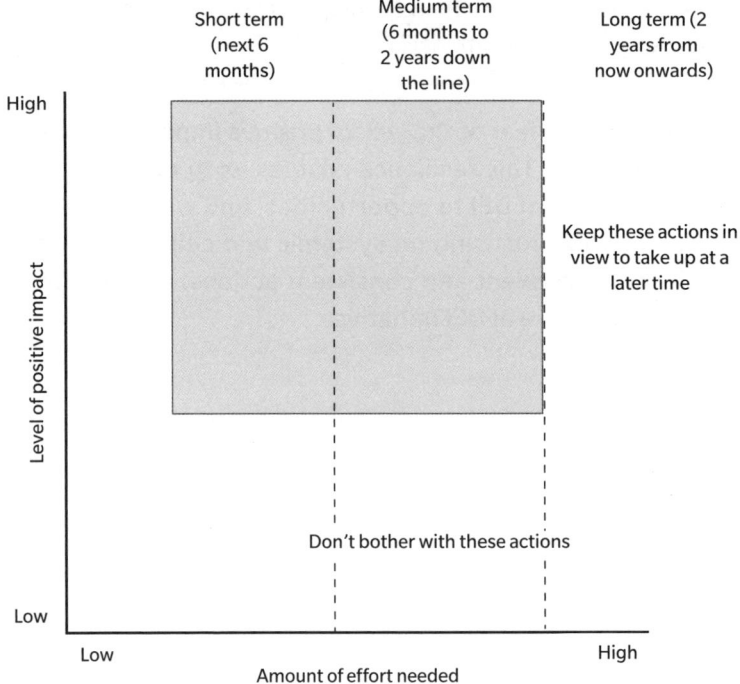

Figure 8.3 Effort vs impact graph with time frames and focus area of actions

time. It is also likely that, with the actions taken in the shaded box, the long-term actions may not require as much effort as you envision today.

- -

Checklist

- -

In your journey in letting go of the fear of a lack of positive impact through resilience have you:

☐ made small efforts to make your workplace more diverse, equitable and inclusive?

☐ identified the activities that you can engage in for systemic and cultural change across your employee life cycle, products and services or marketing and customer service? ➤

☐ built a personal DEI plan to help you focus your efforts for maximising positive impact?

- -

To let go of our fear of the lack of positive impact, we need to be resilient. This resilience enables us to turn the perceived threats of DEI to opportunities, and we can do this with patience, focusing on systemic and cultural change with small, frequent and consistent actions, and trusting the very purpose of DEI initiatives.

Final thoughts: where do we go from here?

'Where are you from?'

That was the opening question from a recent student of mine.

This was not the first time I had been asked that question and, while the question itself seemed innocent, the tone felt otherwise. I have been teaching for over 15 years and have taught thousands of students, but something didn't feel right.

I asked back, 'How does it matter?'

I was not prepared for what was to come.

The student expressed his surprise to see someone 'like me' teaching at the university.

That took me by surprise. I froze.

This comment turned out to be the first of what was to become a series of increasingly aggressive incidents aimed at myself and my course, which was on the topics of inclusive leadership and cross-cultural competency building in global organisations. It ended with threatening behaviour towards me and other students, and the accusation that I was racist towards white men.

The experience shook me to my very core.

I made a conscious choice to enter the field of DEI. I know that there are risks involved in advocating for greater representation, equity and inclusion in our workplaces.

I am not a stranger to verbal backlash, both in person and online. I have always seen it as part of the work and proof that, clearly, more needs to be done.

But never before had I experienced a physical threat where I felt physically unsafe and had to advocate for maintaining my personal space and boundaries.

Over the next few hours after that last incident, I experienced fear like I have never experienced before. The physical reactions were easy enough to recognise, from an increased heart rate to trembling. I locked the car door and stayed away from campus for a few weeks.

What I also noticed were thoughts that reflected a fear of engaging in DEI moving forward. In the immediate days after the last incident, I found myself second-guessing what I said and how I presented DEI-related content in subsequent lectures and workshops. I kept asking myself – *can I say that?* – afraid that what I say could potentially trigger an aggressive reaction in someone in the audience. I was afraid that this experience would change the ways in which I did this work. That made me very uneasy.

I absolutely love what I do. Working in the DEI space is my *ikigai* – it's what I love doing, what the world needs, what I am good at and what I can be paid for. It took me years to find my ikigai but, now that I have it, I was not about to let anyone take it away from me.

I knew that I needed not just to manage and let go of my own fear, but also to address the fears in those who see DEI as a threat.

Going through this frightening experience reinforced my motivation to write this book.

DEI is not a trend and is not a 'passing phase'. The need to feel included and represented, the very things championed by DEI efforts, is a core part of human existence. That won't change. It does seem, however, that DEI needs a rebrand. To reach our goals, to achieve diverse and inclusive workspaces through DEI initiatives, we need to let go of our fears and stop seeing DEI as a threat.

I hope that, in having read this book, the frequency with which you think – *can I say that?* – has reduced. I hope that you have a sense of clarity of what DEI is actually about, and see it as less of a threat. I hope that you are less afraid of engaging in DEI topics and initiatives, and that you are feeling less anxious, worried or hesitant. Instead, I hope that you are feeling more motivated to let go of your own fears about DEI by applying the tools laid out in this book. I do hope that this book has empowered you to bring forth the cultural transformation needed to make our workplaces more diverse, equitable and inclusive.

Drawing on the pioneering work of Daniel Goleman on emotional intelligence, I hope that in reading this book you have become:[231]

- more self-aware of your own emotions, motivators, values and goals when it comes to DEI, and being able to recognise your impact on others,

- better able to self-regulate the emotions and impulses that arise when engaging on DEI topics and initiatives, while being able to suspend judgement by thinking before acting,

- more motivated to do more with a clear sense of purpose and passion towards making our workplaces more diverse, equitable and inclusive,

- more empathetic to consider other people's emotions and perspectives, especially when making decisions,

- more comfortable in your social skills to manage relationships and build networks with people who are different from you.

This emotional intelligence is crucial to driving the cultural transformation that is needed. As you look ahead to continuing your journey to make workplaces more diverse, equitable and inclusive, I would like to offer you my *5R framework*:

Resist the temptation to defend and rationalise. Be aware, stop yourself and disrupt your patterns of behaviour.

Reflect on what you are feeling. Ask yourself: why am I feeling this way? Where is it coming from? Why am I feeling threatened? Go deep with your questions.

Recognise the fear. Name it. Acknowledge it.

Respond to let go of your fear. Be open, curious, vulnerable, courageous and resilient. Act inclusively.

Review your progress and behaviours. Seek feedback for growth.

Change is not straightforward or easy, but change is what is needed to create more diverse, equitable and inclusive workplaces. Learning to recognise our fears and how to let go of them is the first step on a journey towards a more inclusive world. To continue to have a positive impact, we need to take actions to ensure that our culture – and systems, structures, policies and practices – are equitable and inclusive. In wrapping up my final thoughts, I leave you with this quote by Bell Hooks, US author and theorist, 'What we do is more important than what we say or what we say we believe.'

Poornima

Bibliography

1 Adichie, C.N. (2015) *We Should All Be Feminists*. New York: Anchor Books.

2 Schrader, P.G. and Lawless, K. (2004) 'The knowledge, attitudes, & behaviors approach how to evaluate performance and learning in complex environments', *Performance Improvement*, 43, 8–15.

3 Maslow, A.H. (1943) 'A theory of human motivation', *Psychological Review*, 50(4), 370–96. Available at: https://doi.org/10.1037/h0054346.

4 https://online.hbs.edu/blog/post/what-is-dei.

5 Crenshaw, K. (1989) 'Demarginalizing the intersection of race and sex: A black feminist critique of antidiscrimination doctrine, feminist theory and antiracist politics', University of Chicago Legal Forum: vol. 1989, article 8.

6 Crenshaw, K. (1989) 'Demarginalizing the intersection of race and sex: A black feminist critique of antidiscrimination doctrine, feminist theory and antiracist politics', University of Chicago Legal Forum: vol. 1989, article 8.

7 https://online.hbs.edu/blog/post/what-is-dei.

8 https://online.hbs.edu/blog/post/what-is-dei.

9 Shore, L., Randel, A., Chung, B., Dean, M., Ehrhart, K. and Singh, G. (2011) 'Inclusion and diversity in work groups: A review and

model for future research, *Journal of Management*, 37. Available at: https://doi.org/10.1177/0149206310385943.

10 Dhanani, L.Y., Sultan, M., Pham, C.T., Mikami, K., Charles, D.R. and Crandell, H.A. (2024) 'Inclusion near and far: A qualitative investigation of inclusive organizational behavior across work modalities and social identities', *Journal of Organizational Behavior*, 1–18.

11 https://www.bcg.com/publications/2024/four-keys-to-boosting-inclusion-and-beating-burnout.

12 Leslie, L.M. (2019) 'Diversity initiative effectiveness: A typological theory of unintended consequences', *Academy of Management Review*, 44(3), 538–63. Available at: https://doi.org/10.5465/amr.2017.0087.

13 https://www.fastcompany.com/91121256/heres-what-it-feels-like-to-be-used-for-your-companys-stock-photo.

14 https://www.hr-brew.com/stories/2024/02/09/the-majority-85-of-companies-globally-now-have-a-de-and-i-budget-and-nearly-one-half-plan-to-increase-it-in-the-coming-year-survey-finds.

15 https://www.littler.com/publication-press/press/c-suite-executives-committed-inclusion-equity-and-diversity-despite-backlash.

16 https://www.i4cp.com/productivity-blog/whos-challenging-workplace-de-i-efforts-managers

17 https://irp.cdn-website.com/0dd693a6/files/uploaded/Briefing%20-%20Senior%20Executives%20on%20Diversity%20Initiatives%20vEXTERNAL.pdf.

18 https://www.conference-board.org/press/chro-confidence-q4.

19 https://www.bsr.org/en/blog/how-diversity-equity-inclusion-is-gaining-momentum-in-asia-pacific.

20 https://www.bcg.com/publications/2023/taking-diversity-to-the-next-level-in-southeast-asia.

21 Luthra, P. (2021) *Diversifying Diversity: Your Guide to Being an Active Ally of Inclusion in the Workplace*. Denmark: self-published.

22 https://www.kcl.ac.uk/giwl/assets/iwd-2024-survey.pdf.

23 https://fortune.com/2023/01/12/fortune-500-companies-ceos-women-10-percent/; https://www.heidrick.com/-/media/heidrick-com/publications-and-reports/where-are-the-women-ceos.pdf.

24 https://www.spglobal.com/esg/insights/featured/special-editorial/women-in-leadership-what-s-the-holdup.

25 https://www.ndtv.com/education/on-increased-female-enrollment-in-stem-courses-a-thumbs-up-from-experts-4973808.

26 https://www.weforum.org/agenda/2024/03/empowering-women-in-stem-how-we-break-barriers-from-classroom-to-c-suite/.

27 https://www.spglobal.com/esg/insights/featured/special-editorial/women-in-leadership-what-s-the-holdup.

28 Ryan, M.K. and Haslam, S.A. (2005) 'The glass cliff: Evidence that women are over-represented in precarious leadership positions', *British Journal of Management*, 16(2), 81–90. Available at: https://doi.org/10.1111/j.1467-8551.2005.00433.x.

29 https://www.catalyst.org/2024/01/31/glass-cliff-women-of-color/.

30 https://www.russellreynolds.com/en/insights/reports-surveys/global-ceo-turnover-index; https://www.theguardian.com/business/2023/nov/05/over-the-glass-cliff-female-chief-executives-have-shorter-tenure-than-men-due-to-crisis-management-roles.

31 Rosette, A.S. and Livingston, R.W. (2012) 'Failure is not an option for black women: Effects of organizational performance on leaders with single versus dual-subordinate identities', *Journal of Experimental Social Psychology*, 48(5), 1162–7. Available at: https://doi.org/10.1016/j.jesp.2012.05.002.

32 https://hbr.org/podcast/2024/03/why-the-glass-cliff-persists.

33 https://hbr.org/2024/04/more-women-work-in-nonprofits-so-why-do-men-end-up-leading-them.

34 Williams, C.L. (1992) 'The glass escalator: Hidden advantages for men in the "female" professions', *Social Problems*, 39(3), 253–67. Available at: https://doi.org/10.1525/sp.1992.39.3.03x0034h.

35 https://www.mckinsey.com/featured-insights/diversity-and-inclusion/women-in-the-workplace#/.

36 https://www.deloitte.com/global/en/issues/work/content/women-at-work-global-outlook.html

37 https://www.bcg.com/publications/2020/inclusive-cultures-must-follow-new-lgbtq-workforce.

38 https://www.bcg.com/publications/2020/inclusive-cultures-must-follow-new-lgbtq-workforce.

39 https://www.bcg.com/publications/2023/danish-companies-miss-the-mark-on-lgbt-inclusion.

40 https://qnotescarolinas.com/wp-content/uploads/2019/11/Glassdoor-Diversity-Survey-Supplement-1.pdf.

41 https://www.hr-brew.com/stories/2024/09/04/72-of-lgbtq-adults-say-they-would-feel-less-accepted-at-companies-that-roll-back-de-and-i-human-rights-campaign-finds.

42 https://fortune.com/2024/02/09/black-ceos-fortune-500-high-workplace-diversity/.

43 https://fra.europa.eu/en/publication/2023/being-black-eu.

44 European network against racism (ENAR) 'Racism & discrimination in employment in Europe 2013–2017'.

45 Gaddis, S.M. (2017) 'How black are Lakisha and Jamal? Racial perceptions from names used in correspondence audit studies', *Sociological Science*, 4, 469–89. Available at: https://doi.org/10.15195/v4.a19.

46 European network against racism (ENAR) Report 'Racism & discrimination in employment in Europe 2013–2017'.

47 Kang, S., Decelles, K., Tilcsik, A. and Jun, S. (2016) 'Whitened resumés: Race and self-presentation in the labor market', *Administrative Science Quarterly*, 61. Available at: https://doi.org/10.1177/0001839216639577.

48 https://www-bbc-com.cdn.ampproject.org/c/s/www.bbc.com/news/uk-63494849.amp.

49 https://www2.deloitte.com/content/dam/Deloitte/us/
Documents/about-deloitte/inclusion-survey-research-the-bias-
barrier.pdf.

50 Buttigieg, D. (2011) 'The business case for an age-diverse work-
force' in: Parry, E. and Tyson, S. (eds) *Managing an Age-Diverse
Workforce*. Palgrave Macmillan: London. Available at: https://doi.
org/10.1057/9780230299115_2; Cutcher, L., Riach, K. and Tyler,
M. (2022) 'Splintering organizational subjectivities: Older workers and the dynamics of recognition, vulnerability and resistance',
Organization Studies, 43(6), 973–92; Li, Y., Gong, Y., Burmeister,
A., Wang, M., Alterman, V., Alonso, A. and Robinson, S. (2021)
'Leveraging age diversity for organizational performance: An
intellectual capital perspective', *Journal of Applied Psychology*,
106(1), 71.

51 Posthuma, R.A., Wagstaff, M.F. and Campion, M.A. (2012) 'Age
stereotypes and workplace age discrimination: A framework for
future research' in Borman, W.C. and Hedge, J.W. (eds) *The Oxford
Handbook of Work and Aging*, Oxford Library of Psychology (online
edn, Oxford Academic, 18 September 2012). Available at: https://
doi.org/10.1093/oxfordhb/9780195385052.013.0104; Riach, K.
(2009) 'Managing "difference": Understanding age diversity in
practice', *Human Resource Management Journal*, 19(3), 319–35.

52 https://qnotescarolinas.com/wp-content/uploads/2019/11/
Glassdoor-Diversity-Survey-Supplement-1.pdf.

53 https://newsroom.accenture.com/news/2018/companies-
leading-in-disability-inclusion-have-outperformed-peers-
accenture-research-finds.

54 https://www.thehindu.com/opinion/op-ed/investing-in-persons-
with-disabilities/article68566214.ece.

55 https://documents.worldbank.org/en/publication/documents-
reports/documentdetail/358151468268839622/people-with-
disabilities-in-india-from-commitments-to-outcomes.

56 https://economictimes.indiatimes.com/jobs/hr-policies-trends/
top-indian-companies-have-very-few-people-with-disabilities-on-
rolls/articleshow/102753098.cms?from=mdr.

57 Office of National Statistics: https://www.ons.gov.uk/.

58 Crenshaw, K. (1989) 'Demarginalizing the intersection of race and sex: A black feminist critique of antidiscrimination doctrine, feminist theory and antiracist politics', University of Chicago Legal Forum: vol. 1989, article 8.

59 https://www.catalyst.org/reports/antiracism-workplace-leadership/.

60 https://www.deloitte.com/global/en/issues/work/content/women-at-work-global-outlook.html.

61 https://www.deloitte.com/global/en/issues/work/content/women-at-work-global-outlook.html.

62 https://www.ddiworld.com/glf/diversity-equity-inclusion-report-2023/company-dei-practices.

63 https://www2.deloitte.com/us/en/insights/focus/human-capital-trends.html.

64 https://twitter.com/elonmusk/status/1735568882499211557?lang=en.

65 https://twitter.com/elonmusk/status/1735568882499211557?lang=en.

66 https://edition.cnn.com/2024/01/04/business/lululemon-founder-dei-chip-wilson/index.html.

67 https://www.nbcnews.com/news/nbcblk/diversity-roles-disappear-three-years-george-floyd-protests-inspired-rcna72026.

68 https://www.forbes.com/sites/forbeshumanresourcescouncil/2023/06/29/dei-progress-is-facing-a-concerning-reversal/.

69 https://news.bloomberglaw.com/daily-labor-report/corporate-diversity-pledges-fizzle-amid-layoffs-gop-backlash.

70 https://edition.cnn.com/2024/01/07/us/dei-attacks-experts-warn-of-consequences-reaj/index.html.

71 https://www.independent.co.uk/business/kemi-badenoch-diversity-initiatives-can-be-ineffective-and-counterproductive-b2515403.html.

72 https://www.telegraph.co.uk/news/2024/04/19/im-a-woman-of-colour-dei-is-just-woke-propaganda/.

73 https://www.foxbusiness.com/media/alleged-insider-says-boeings-woes-symptom-failure-elites-dei-ripping-society-apart.

74 https://www.msn.com/en-us/money/companies/elon-musk-blames-diversity-efforts-for-the-widespread-crowdstrike-digital-pandemic-that-stunted-microsoft-services/ar-BB1qkDlI.

75 https://www.reuters.com/world/us/trump-vows-fight-anti-white-feeling-us-his-allies-have-plan-2024-05-04/.

76 https://www.nbcnews.com/news/nbcblk/kamala-harris-labeled-dei-candidate-makes-latest-recipient-emerging-in-rcna163842.

77 https://www.bloomberg.com/news/articles/2024-08-19/harley-drops-diversity-initiatives-maligned-by-anti-dei-activist?.

78 https://www.bloomberg.com/opinion/articles/2024-08-21/harley-davidson-drops-dei-as-right-pushes-to-get-politics-out-of-business?.

79 https://press.un.org/en/2023/gashc4393.doc.htm.

80 https://www.bbc.com/news/articles/ckg55we5n3xo.

81 https://www.ft.com/content/c975fc2c-e6b9-402d-baa6-d87f036fc1d3.

82 https://www.reuters.com/markets/europe/german-ceos-warn-far-right-threat-economy-2024-01-17/.

83 https://www.nzherald.co.nz/nz/universitys-action-of-having-segregated-areas-for-maori-and-pasifika-students-comparable-to-ku-klux-klan-says-winston-peters/KU6GIWYPE5CZDIVA67EWMXETCA/.

84 https://www.bbc.com/news/world-australia-68770187.

85 https://www.aljazeera.com/news/2024/2/26/hamas-to-halal-how-anti-muslim-hate-speech-is-spreading-in-india#:~:.

86 https://www.npr.org/2024/07/22/nx-s1-5043751/france-olympics-hijab-ban-amnesty-international.

87 https://www.theguardian.com/society/2023/oct/05/record-rise-hate-crimes-transgender-people-reported-england-and-wales.

88 https://www.hindustantimes.com/trending/ola-ceo-bhavish-aggarwal-terms-gender-pronouns-as-illness-internet-is-disappointed-disgusted-101714985725192.html.

89 https://www.ft.com/content/29fd9b5c-2f35-41bf-9d4c-994db4e12998.

90 https://www.theguardian.com/society/2024/feb/03/andrew-tate-symptom-not-problem-why-young-men-turning-against-feminism.

91 https://www.ft.com/content/1843b68e-64cf-479f-b354-a7081257d42e.

92 https://www.fastcompany.com/91154675/shrm-hr-organization-dropped-equity-from-dei.

93 https://www.i4cp.com/productivity-blog/whos-challenging-workplace-de-i-efforts-managers.

94 Nittrouer, C.L., Arena, D. Jr, Silver, E.R., Avery, D.R. and Hebl, M.R. (2024) 'Despite the haters: The immense promise and progress of diversity, equity, and inclusion initiatives', *Journal of Organizational Behavior*, 1–14. Available at: https://doi-org.esc-web.lib.cbs.dk/10.1002/job.2835.

95 Plummer, D.L. (1998) 'Approaching diversity training in the year 2000', *Consulting Psychology Journal: Practice and Research*, 50(3), 181–9.

96 Ruggs, E., Summerville, K. and Marshburn, C. (2020) 'The response to social justice issues in organizations as a form of diversity resistance', in Thomas, K. (ed.) *Diversity Resistance in Organizations*. Routledge. Available at: https://doi.org/10.4324/9781003026907-7.

97 Velasco, M. and Sansone, C. (2019) 'Resistance to diversity and inclusion change initiatives: Strategies for transformational leaders', *Organization Development Journal*, 37, 9–20.

98 Velasco, M. and Sansone, C. (2019) 'Resistance to diversity and inclusion change initiatives: Strategies for transformational leaders', *Organization Development Journal*, 37, 9–20.

99 https://www.wsj.com/articles/bud-light-boycott-sales-dylan-mulvaney-6c23bb86.

100 https://www.barrons.com/articles/bud-light-sales-dylan-mulvaney-transgender-backlash-9d426f09; https://edition.cnn.com/2023/04/26/business/bud-light-distributors-response/index.html.

101 https://www.nytimes.com/2023/07/23/business/modelo-bud-light.html.

102 https://www.nytimes.com/2023/05/25/business/target-pride-lgbtq-companies-backlash.html.

103 Velasco, M. and Sansone, C. (2019) 'Resistance to diversity and inclusion change initiatives: Strategies for transformational leaders', *Organization Development Journal*, 37, 9–20.

104 https://www.washingtonpost.com/business/2024/02/20/corporate-diversity-job-cuts/.

105 https://www.linkedin.com/pulse/whos-vaulting-c-suite-trends-changed-fast-2022-george-anders/.

106 https://www.glassdoor.com/research/who-cares-about-diversity-equity-and-inclusion.

107 https://www.bloomberg.com/news/articles/2024-04-18/bosses-across-corporate-america-squeeze-in-house-affinity-groups-in-dei-retreat.

108 https://www.forbes.com/sites/forbesbusinesscouncil/2022/12/30/four-reasons-to-prioritize-dei-during-a-recession/.

109 https://hbr.org/2024/01/why-dei-leaders-are-burning-out-and-how-organizations-can-help.

110 Weeks, K.P., Taylor, N., Hall, A.V., Bell, M.P., Nottingham, A. and Evans, L. (2024) '"They say they support diversity initiatives, but they don't demonstrate it": The impact of DEI paradigms on the emotional labor of HR&DEI professionals', *Journal of Business Psychology*, 39, 411–33. Available at: https://doi.org/10.1007/s10869-023-09886-8.

111 https://www.axios.com/2024/04/19/jamie-dimon-dei-jpmorgan.

112 https://gusto.com/company-news/a-real-time-look-at-the-great-resignation-january-2022#Quits_by_Gender.

113 Parker, K. and Horowitz, J.M. (2022) 'Majority of workers who quit a job in 2021 cite low pay, no opportunities for advancement, feeling disrespected', Pew Research Center, 9 March.

114 https://sloanreview.mit.edu/article/toxic-culture-is-driving-the-great-resignation/.

115 https://www.ddiworld.com/glf/diversity-equity-inclusion-report-2023/diversity-retention.

116 https://ellafwashington.com/not-everyone-can-quiet-quit-2/.

117 https://www.gallup.com/workplace/349484/state-of-the-global-workplace.aspx#ite-506924.

118 https://www.forbes.com/sites/allbusiness/2022/12/19/quiet-quitting-is-a-sign-of-a-deeper-problem-heres-what-it-means/; https://fortune.com/2023/02/28/conscious-quitting-leaders/.

119 https://fortune.com/2023/02/28/conscious-quitting-leaders/.

120 https://fortune.com/2022/11/29/what-is-career-cushioning-job-hunting-amid-recession-fears/

121 https://ellafwashington.com/not-everyone-can-quiet-quit-2/.

122 https://www.cnbc.com/2023/02/28/half-of-black-workers-want-to-quitheres-what-companies-can-do-better.html.

123 https://www.indeed.com/career-advice/news/black-workers-consider-leaving-job.

124 US Civil Rights Commission (1977) Authorization Act. 95th Congress. Available at: https://www.aaaed.org/aaaed/About_Affirmative_Action__Diversity_and_Inclusion.asp#:~:text=-Affirmative%20action%20itself%20has%20been,Statement%20on%20Affirmative%20Action%2C%20October.

125 Nittrouer, C.L., Arena, D. Jr, Silver, E.R., Avery, D.R. and Hebl, M.R. (2024) 'Despite the haters: The immense promise and

progress of diversity, equity, and inclusion initiatives', *Journal of Organizational Behavior*, 1–14. Available at: https://doi-org.esc-web.lib.cbs.dk/10.1002/job.2835.

126 https://www.merriam-webster.com/dictionary/meritocracy#:~:.

127 www.bbc.com/news/articles/c8rxvd2z6ldo.amp.

128 https://hbr.org/2022/06/stop-making-the-business-case-for-diversity.

129 https://twitter.com/elonmusk/status/1735568882499211557?lang=en.

130 https://hbr.org/2023/03/to-overcome-resistance-to-dei-understand-whats-driving-it; Shuman, E., Van Zomeren, M., Saguy, T. and Knowles, E. (2022) 'Defend, deny, distance, and dismantle: A measure of how advantaged group members manage their identity', Available at: https://doi.org/10.31234/osf.io/6d4qc; Plaut, V., Romano, C., Hurd, K. and Goldstein, E. (2020) 'Diversity resistance redux in diversity resistance in organizations', in Thomas, K. (ed.) *Diversity Resistance in Organizations*. Routledge. Available at: https://doi.org/10.4324/9781003026907-6.

131 Luthra, P. (2022) *The Art of Active Allyship*. Denmark: TalentED.

132 Plaut, V., Romano, C., Hurd, K. and Goldstein, E. (2020) 'Diversity resistance redux in diversity resistance in organizations', in Thomas, K. (ed.) *Diversity Resistance in Organizations*. Routledge. Available at: https://doi.org/ 10.4324/9781003026907-6.

133 Plaut, V., Romano, C., Hurd, K. and Goldstein, E. (2020) 'Diversity resistance redux in diversity resistance in organizations', in Thomas, K. (ed.) *Diversity Resistance in Organizations*. Routledge. Available at: https://doi.org/ 10.4324/9781003026907-6.

134 Plaut, V., Romano, C., Hurd, K. and Goldstein, E. (2020) 'Diversity resistance redux in diversity resistance in organizations', in Thomas, K. (ed.) *Diversity Resistance in Organizations*. Routledge. Available at: https://doi.org/ 10.4324/9781003026907-6.

135 Danbold, F. and Huo, Y.J. (2015) 'No longer "all-American"? Whites' defensive reactions to their numerical decline', *Social*

Psychological and Personality Science, 6(2), 210–18. Available at: https://doi.org/10.1177/1948550614546355.

136 https://hbr.org/2023/03/to-overcome-resistance-to-dei-understand-whats-driving-it.

137 Velasco, M. and Sansone, C. (2019) 'Resistance to diversity and inclusion change initiatives: Strategies for transformational leaders', *Organization Development Journal*, 37, 9–20.

138 Velasco, M. and Sansone, C. (2019) 'Resistance to diversity and inclusion change initiatives: Strategies for transformational leaders', *Organization Development Journal*, 37, 9–20.

139 Muo, I. (2014) 'The other side of change resistance', *International Review of Management and Business Research*, 3, 96–112.

140 Velasco, M. and Sansone, C. (2019) 'Resistance to diversity and inclusion change initiatives: Strategies for transformational leaders', *Organization Development Journal*, 37, 9–20.

141 Plutchik, R. (1980) 'A general psychoevolutionary theory of emotion' in Plutchik, R. and Kellerman, H. (eds) *Emotion: Theory, Research and Experience: Theories of Emotion*. New York: Academic Press, vol. 1, pp. 3–33; Plutchik, R. (1982) 'A psychoevolutionary theory of emotions', *Social Science Information*, 21(4–5), 529–53. Available at: https://doi.org/10.1177/053901882021004003.

142 https://www.psychologytoday.com/us/blog/overcoming-destructive-anger/202103/fear-and-anger-similarities-differences-and-interaction.

143 Ekman, P. (1999) 'Basic emotions' in Dalgleish, T. and Power, M. (eds) *'Handbook of Cognition and Emotion*. Sussex: John Wiley & Sons.

144 Plutchik, R. (2001) 'The nature of emotions', *American Scientist*, 89, 344–50. Available at: https://doi.org/10.1511/2001.28.344.

145 Cowen, A.S. and Keltner, D. (2017) 'Self-report captures 27 distinct categories of emotion bridged by continuous gradients', Proceedings of the National Academy of Sciences of the United States of America, 114(38), E7900–E7909. Available at: https://doi.org/10.1073/pnas.1702247114.

146 https://feelingswheel.com/.

147 Cannon, W.B. (1915) *Bodily Changes in Pain, Hunger, Fear and Rage*. New York: D. Appleton & Company.

148 Walker, P. (2013) *Complex PTSD: From Surviving to Thriving: A Guide and Map for Recovering from Childhood Trauma*. An Azure Coyote Book; Donahue, J.J. (2020) 'Fight-flight-freeze system' in Zeigler-Hill, V. and Shackelford, T.K. (eds) *Encyclopedia of Personality and Individual Differences*, pp. 1590–5. Available at: https://doi.org/10.1007/978-3-319-24612-3_751; Bracha, H.S. (2004) 'Freeze, flight, fight, fright, faint: Adaptationist perspectives on the acute stress response spectrum', CNS Spectrums, October, 9(9), 679–85. Available at: https://doi.org/10.1017/S1092852900001954.

149 https://www.forbes.com/sites/jackkelly/2023/07/17/the-negative-impact-of-toxic-positivity-in-the-workplace/.

150 https://www.psychologytoday.com/us/basics/toxic-positivity.

151 Goodman, W. (2022) *Toxic Positivity: How to Embrace Every Emotion in a Happy-Obsessed World*. Orion Publishing Group Limited.

152 https://www.valuescentre.com/resources.

153 https://www.valuescentre.com/resources.

154 https://www.i4cp.com/productivity-blog/whos-challenging-workplace-de-i-efforts-managers.

155 Thaler, R. and Sunstein, C. (2008) *Nudge: Improving Decisions about Health, Wealth, and Happiness*. New Haven: Yale University Press.

156 Thaler, R. and Sunstein, C. (2008) *Nudge: Improving Decisions about Health, Wealth, and Happiness*. New Haven: Yale University Press.

157 Ferguson, S. (2014) 'Privilege 101: A quick and dirty guide', *Everyday Feminism*, 29 September. Available at: https://everydayfeminism.com/2014/09/what-is-privilege/; McIntosh, P. (1989) *White Privilege: Unpacking the Invisible Knapsack*. Peace and Freedom, pp. 10–12.

158 https://libguides.lib.msu.edu/c.php?g=1133877&p=8276231.

159 https://www.merriam-webster.com/dictionary/power.

160 Joy, M. (2023) *How to End Injustice Everywhere: Understanding the Common Denominator Driving All Injustices, to Create a Better World for Humans, Animals, and the Planet.* Lantern Publishing & Media.

161 Williams, J.C. (2021) *Bias Interrupted: Creating Inclusion for Real and for Good.* Boston Harvard Business Press.

162 LeanIn.Org and McKinsey & Company, 'Women in the Workplace 2019'.

163 Luthra, P. and Muhr, S.L. (2023) *Leading through Bias: 5 Essential Skills to Block Bias and Improve Inclusion at Work.* Palgrave Executive Essentials. Available at: https://doi.org/10.1007/978-3-031-38571-1_1.

164 https://www.dictionary.com/browse/toxic-masculinity

165 https://fortune.com/2024/02/06/working-fathers-microaggressions-daddy-tracked-careers

166 https://hdr.undp.org/content/ 2023-gender-social-norms-index-gsni#/indicies/GSNI.

167 https://www.otheringandbelonging.org/the-problem-of-othering/.

168 https://hbr.org/2024/03/how-to-build-a-broader-network-within-your-company.

169 Hamilton, R., Mittal, C., Shah, A., Thompson, D.V. and Griskevicius, V. (2019) 'How financial constraints influence consumer behavior: An integrative framework', *Journal of Consumer Psychology*, 29(2), 285–305.

170 https://www.womenofinfluence.ca/tps/.

171 https://www.fastcompany.com/91113957/4-common-arguments-against-dei-and-how-to-dismantle-each-one.

172 https://www.fastcompany.com/91113957/4-common-arguments-against-dei-and-how-to-dismantle-each-one.

173 Homan, A.C. (2019) 'Dealing with diversity in workgroups: Preventing problems and promoting potential', *Social and Personality Psychology Compass*, 13(5). Available at: https://doi.org/10.1111/spc3.12465.

174 Reynolds, A. and Lewis, D. (2017) 'Teams solve problems faster when they're more cognitively diverse, *Harvard Business Review*, 30 March.

175 Corritore, M., Goldberg, A. and Srivastava, S.B. (2020) 'The new analytics of culture', *Harvard Business Review*, January–February.

176 Travis, D.J., Shaffer, E. and Thorpe-Moscon, J. (2019) *Getting Real about Inclusive Leadership: Why Change Starts with You.* Catalyst.

177 International Labor Organization (2019) 'Women in business and management: The business case for change', p. 21.

178 Bourke, J. and Espedido, A. (2019) 'Why inclusive leaders are good for organisations, and how to become one', *Harvard Business Review*, 29 March.

179 European Commission (2016) 'The business case for diversity in the workplace: Sexual orientation and gender identity. Report on good practices', 26 September. Available at: https://www.raznolikost.eu/wp-content/uploads/The-buisiness-case-for-diversity.pdf.

180 https://www.dol.gov/.

181 https://www.business.com/articles/hire-disabled-people/.

182 McCallaghan, S., Jackson, L.T.B. and Heyns, M.M. (2019) 'Examining the mediating effect of diversity climate on the relationship between destructive leadership and employee attitudes', *Journal of Psychology in Africa*, 29(6), 563–9; Perry, E.L. and Li, A. (2020) 'Diversity climate in organisations' in *Oxford Research Encyclopedia of Business and Management.* Oxford University Press.

183 Tuan, L.T., Rowley, C. and Thao, V.T. (2019) 'Addressing employee diversity to foster their work engagement', *Journal of Business Research*, 95, 303–15.

184 Travis, D.J., Shaffer, E. and Thorpe-Moscon, J. (2019) *Getting Real about Inclusive Leadership: Why Change Starts with You*. Catalyst.

185 https://www.merriam-webster.com/dictionary/gaslighting.

186 https://www.monster.com/.

187 Criado Perez, C. (2019) *Invisible Women: Exposing Data Bias in a World Designed for Men*. Harry N. Abrams.

188 Yoshino, K. (2006) *Covering: The Hidden Assault on Our Civil Rights* (1st ed.). Random House.

189 Hedberg, B.L.T. (1981) 'How organisations learn and unlearn' in Nystrom, P.C. and Starbuck, W.H. (eds) *Handbook of Organisational Design* (1, 3–27). New York: Oxford University Press.

190 Klein, J. (1989) 'Parenthetic learning in organisations: Toward the unlearning of the unlearning model', *Journal of Management Studies*, 26, 291–308.

191 https://hbr.org/2022/03/do-your-global-teams-see-dei-as-an-american-issue.

192 https://www.economist.com/the-economist-explains/2021/07/30/how-has-the-meaning-of-the-word-woke-evolved.

193 https://www.merriam-webster.com/dictionary/woke.

194 https://www.mckinsey.com/featured-insights/diversity-and-inclusion/women-in-the-workplace.

195 Jones, K.P., Peddie, C.I., Gilrane, V.L., King, E.B. and Gray, A.L. (2016) 'Not so subtle: A meta-analytic investigation of the correlates of subtle and overt discrimination', *Journal of Management*, 42(6), 1588–613.

196 https://hbr.org/2022/05/research-the-real-time-impact-of-microaggressions.

197 https://hbr.org/2022/03/we-need-to-retire-the-term-microaggressions.

198 https://hbr.org/2022/03/we-need-to-retire-the-term-microaggressions.

199 https://hbr.org/2022/03/we-need-to-retire-the-term-microaggressions.

200 https://wiw-report.s3.amazonaws.com/Women_in_the_
Workplace_2016.pdf; https://www.forbes.com/sites/
darreonnadavis/2022/06/15/black-women-are-less-likely-
to-get-quality-feedback-at-work-that-impacts-their-earnings-
and-leadership-opportunities-over-time/.

201 https://hbr.org/2001/04/race-matters.

202 https://chief.com/articles/feedback-style.

203 https://www.thetimes.co.uk/article/death-of-the-chairman-
city-switching-to-more-inclusive-chairs-m97gbff2c.

204 https://www.iamnotatypo.org/.

205 Edmondson, A. (2023) *Right Kind of Wrong: Why Learning to Fail
Can Teach Us to Thrive*. New York: Atria Books.

206 Edmondson A. (2023) *Right Kind of Wrong: Why Learning to Fail
Can Teach Us to Thrive*. New York: Atria Books.

207 Edmondson, A. (1999) 'Psychological safety and learning behavior in teams', *Administrative Science Quarterly*, 44, 250–82.

208 https://hbr.org/2016/01/what-having-a-growth-mindset-actu-
ally-means.

209 https://upcurrent.beehiiv.com/p/how-to-identify-and-avoid-
channel-switching-in-conversations-about-race?utm_con-
tent=294246559&utm_medium=social&utm_source=linked-
in&hss_channel=lis-reQWtZWLhQ.

210 https://www.forbes.com/sites/sujanpatel/2016/03/09/why-
feeling-uncomfortable-is-the-key-to-success/?sh=19a617aa1913.

211 https://www.reuters.com/world/us/trump-vows-fight-anti-
white-feeling-us-his-allies-have-plan-2024-05-04/?utm_
source=Sailthru&utm_medium=Newsletter&utm_campaign=
Weekend-Briefing&utm_term=050424&user_.

212 Luthra, P. and Muhr, S.L. (2023) *Leading through Bias: 5
Essential Skills to Block Bias and Improve Inclusion at Work*.
Palgrave Executive Essentials. Available at: https://doi.
org/10.1007/978-3-031-38571-1_1.

213 https://sloanreview.mit.edu/article/how-a-values-based-approach-advances-dei/.

214 https://hbr.org/2024/07/what-sets-genius-teams-apart.

215 https://fortune.com/2023/01/06/kinkeeping-what-it-means-tiktok-viral/.

216 https://theinclusionsolution.me/managing-the-toll-of-dei-work-dissecting-the-emotional-toll-and-fatigue-of-dei-work/.

217 Smith, J.L., McPartlan, P., Poe, J. and Thoman, D.B. (2021) 'Diversity fatigue: A survey for measuring attitudes towards diversity enhancing efforts in academia', *Cultural Diversity and Ethnic Minority Psychology*, 27(4), 659–74. Available at: https://doi.org/10.1037/cdp0000406.

218 https://www.medicalnewstoday.com/articles/weathering-what-are-the-health-effects-of-stress-and-discrimination.

219 Geronimus, A., Hicken, M., Keene, D. and Bound, J. (2006) '"Weathering" and age patterns of allostatic load scores among blacks and whites in the United States', *American Journal of Public Health*, 96, 826–33. Available at: https://doi.org/ 10.2105/ AJPH.2004.060749.

220 https://hbr.org/2024/01/why-dei-leaders-are-burning-out-and-how-organizations-can-help; Grandey, A.A. (2003) 'When "the show must go on": Surface acting and deep acting as determinants of emotional exhaustion and peer-rated service delivery. *The Academy of Management Journal*, 46(1), 86–96.

221 https://hbr.org/2024/01/why-dei-leaders-are-burning-out-and-how-organizations-can-help; Ashforth, B.E. and Humphrey, R.H. (1993) 'Emotional labor in service roles: The influence of identity', *The Academy of Management Review*, 18(1), 88–115. Available at: https://doi.org/10.2307/258824.

222 Weeks, K.P., Taylor, N., Hall, A.V., Bell, M.P., Nottingham, A. and Evans, L. (2024) '"They say they support diversity initiatives, but they don't demonstrate it": The impact of DEI paradigms on the emotional labor of HR&DEI professionals', *Journal of Business and Psychology*, 39, 411–33. Available at: https://doi.org/10.1007/s10869-023-09886-8.

223 https://www.forbes.com/sites/forbescoachescouncil/2023/11/21/protecting-dei-leaders-mental-health-in-a-challenging-role/.

224 Barker, M.J. (2020) *Gender: A Graphic Guide*. Icon Books Limited.

225 https://mitmgmtfaculty.mit.edu/mrowe/micro-inequities/.

226 Muragishi, G.A., Aguilar, L., Carr, P.B. and Walton, G.M. (2024) 'Microinclusions: Treating women as respected work partners increases a sense of fit in technology companies', *Journal of Personality and Social Psychology*, 126(3), 431–60. Available at: https://doi.org/10.1037/pspi0000430.

227 https://hbr.org/2023/05/an-antidote-to-microaggressions-microvalidations.

228 https://hbr.org/2023/05/an-antidote-to-microaggressions-microvalidations.

229 https://hbr.org/2021/06/dont-just-mentor-women-and-people-of-color-sponsor-them.

230 Scharte, B. (2024) 'Discussing trust and resilience: The need for a healthy dose of distrust', *Risk Hazards & Crisis in Public Policy*. Available at: https://doi.org/10.1002/rhc3.12287.

231 https://hbr.org/2004/01/what-makes-a-leader.

Index

JOIN THE PEARSON BUSINESS BOOK CLUB

> FREE Monthly Webinars with expert authors to help boost your personal and professional development

Discover Now